This is the second volume of Anna Koffer's Stories. She published her first volume in 2 pseudonym Helena Zelená. Her second volume has the same format: it is a mosaic of **very personal** stories that are loosely based on her own experiences: childhood in socialist Czechoslovakia, adult life in London, motherhood, scientific career, travels, and her recent move to mid Wales. Anna never stops wondering about relationships within the family, and those with friends, men, scientific colleagues, food, and even molecules. In her stories, she tries to capture some pivotal moments of a life that coincided with some of the most dramatic social and political upheavals of the past decades. The stories are listed chronologically - the dates relate to the years when the events took place and not to the time of writing.

Anna Koffer was born in London. Her Jewish parents had spent the war years in England and returned to Prague just after the war had ended. Anna grew up in Prague but emigrated to England in 1968 after Czechoslovakia had been invaded by the Soviet Bloc countries. She worked as a lecturer and a cell biologist until her retirement. Anna lived in London for half a century but has recently moved to Wales to be close to her two sons. She has three grandchildren whose paintings are shown on the book cover.

Copyright © 2024 by Anna Koffer

All rights reserved. This book or any portion thereof may not be reproduced or used in any manner whatsoever without the express written permission of the publisher except for the use of brief quotations in a book review.

First Printing, 2024

ISBN: 9798353836544

To Lokadhi
with love
Anna

Long Life in Short Stories Volume 2

Anna Koffer

For my family and my friends

My heartfelt thanks to Fern Bryant and Birte Pedersen
for their invaluable
friendship, feedback, and encouragement.

CONTENTS

Introduction		7
The Home Journey	1945	11
Methuselah	3 billion years ago	14
Visiting Professor Kohn	1952	18
Always Ready	1953 - 1962	23
Elisa's Loneliness	1960 – 1991 - 1995	30
Posh Cars	1961 - 2012	34
David's Story	1968 - 1977	39
Two Teenagers and Big Mama	1988	46
Muscle Contractions	1993	51
Mission Impossible	1994	60
Fifty	1995	70
A Heavy Shower	2009	74
Uncle Bob's Visit	2014	80
Holiday Fellows	2015	92
Something Uplifting	2016	104
Rosh Hashanah	2017	110
Not Managing	2017	116
Our friend Ivan	2018	121
Pepi's Elegy	2018	128
Café Society	2019	136
The Lycian Way	2019	140
Family Reunion 2020	2020	148
A Moving Story	2020 - 2021	154
A Beautiful Forest	2022	168
Autumn in Llanidloes	2023	172

INTRODUCTION

The stories in this book present an extension of the first volume of "Long Life in Short Stories." They describe events in my life, moderately fictionalised, and are listed chronologically.

For this introduction, however, I take the liberty to use a story written by my father Ernest in May or June 1945 when, after six years of exile in England, he returned to liberated Czechoslovakia. He came as a member of a team of volunteer doctors who went to Terezin Camp to help deal with the typhus epidemic there.

My parents' emigration in 1939 and their subsequent return enabled and determined my existence and my identity. I grew up in the Prague, gradually awakening, in that magical city, to the hypocrisy of the socialist regime. I had two idealist communist parents who both worked very hard. My mother was a pediatrician and my father was a scientist. He was devoted to his research on nerve–muscle interaction. In the 1960s, he gained recognition from and established contacts with many researchers abroad.

History repeats itself. The political situation in 1968, after the Soviet invasion of Czechoslovakia, led to my emigration to England. My parents considered the second exile very seriously but decided against it in the end. Or rather, my father decided. Perhaps, he could not have foreseen the consequences, or perhaps he just could not bring himself to leave his country again.

Before the invasion, during the so-called "Prague Spring", my father signed an article demanding reforms of the regime. It was called "2000 words." After the invasion, a period called "normalisation" started. It was meant to bring things back under Soviet control with the help of a puppet government. The normalising authorities required, among many other measures, that all the signatories renounce their signatures. My father refused and thus became a black sheep. Endless restrictions followed on travel, publishing, lecturing, contacts, and so on. And he was being kept on tenterhooks about whether the normalisers would allow him to continue with his research; he could hardly imagine his life without it. Thus, he lived through nine stressful years of uncertainty.

In the summer of 1977, after a long series of deferential requests and humiliating negotiations, my father was finally allowed by the authorities to come to London together with my mother. It would be the first time he could see his two grandsons, then two and four years old. After two happy weeks in London, spent with us and with his old friends, my father suddenly died of coronary thrombosis. It happened on our way back to London from Cambridge, where we had just visited his scientific friend and colleague.

After my father's death, my mother sent me his diaries, dating from 1945 until the very end, the summer of 1977. I have used some of that material in my previous collection of short stories (in the story "Ernest normalised"). But there is so much more in these diaries, and I felt they should be available not just to me, but to anybody interested in the circumstances of a middle-European idealist of the 1940s turning gradually into a disillusioned observer of the 1970s moral decline in the so-called socialist society. The society that he had once, long ago, so much hoped to help building.

And so, I have scanned and/or digitalised all his diaries and given them to an archive in Prague for future reference. Most texts were in English, some in German, and some in Czech. There was also a set of letters from my father to a Russian scientist. After his death, she sent them to me via a mutual Russian friend who came to London. The letters were written in Russian and in English and dealt mostly with the science of neuro-muscular interaction. They impressed me with their politeness, respect, and friendship, and with their eagerness for an opinion exchange - the possibility of which was so mindlessly curtailed.

It was sad to follow my father's transformation towards pessimism, initially reluctant but then more and more angry and cynical. The loss of trust in relationships with colleagues, the growth of tiredness from the constant uncertainty about his career, but also the determination to carry on regardless. As if he wanted to show them "I don't need you!"

While a writer or a painter can at least write or paint quietly at home, although unpublished, a scientist needs a lab, equipment, discussion, and exchange of ideas. All this was relentlessly controlled by the normalisers and so his work was greatly dependent on their whims. The constant stress took its toll.

But I want to go back to those early idealistic and hopeful years. It seems fitting to start this second collection of my stories with the "Home Journey." It is a story written by my father when he returned to his country. He came to Terezin, so very near to his birthplace, Ústí nad Labem (Aussig an der Elbe in German). It must have been a shock to witness the horrors of the camp and to search in vain for the missing family. But the story is full of hope for a new and better world.

THE HOME JOURNEY
By Ernest Gutmann
1945

How strangely banal is the journey home! When remembered, it comes to you as a charming old folk song. Repetitive, almost boring, but always with the same insistent force. Even the din of the train that's taking you home has a peculiar, singular melody. Its crescendo is getting more and more intensive and clear.

Here they are - the mountains of your country! You are getting up, leaving your compartment, and approaching the window. So here we are again! In front of you lies that grey-blue thread of the river, with mountains gently sloping towards its banks.

You turn around. Maybe some kind of foreigner is standing right behind you and would dearly like to know something about those mountains, about this place. But what's the point? What would the name of a mountain or a village tell him? Maybe you don't even remember these names anymore, maybe you haven't ever known them. Yet you understand quite clearly that this is your country.

The train clamors on, its melody more insistent and significant, and the first houses now appear along its track. Casually, hands in your pockets, you return to your compartment as if to say: "Oh yes, I need to get off at the next stop! Further on, there is nothing attractive for me anymore." Quickly!! Put on your hat and coat, take out your luggage. Your town can be seen behind the window already. Brakes, a little bump - and the journey is over.

One more brief look into the compartment meaning: "I am getting off here, you see, that's where I am from my dear folks!" Mustn't push! One has to get off slowly when arriving home! You aim directly for the exit and the stairs leading down. Maybe someone is waiting, maybe not? Suddenly in the sea of indifferent eyes, an intimately known face may appear.

One thing, however, is certain. The familiar Station Square awaits you outside. Very well, very well, here is that narrow station alleyway that obstructs the traffic! It belongs to this town just like its air, not different from any other town but still quite special. You can hear the familiar sound of the trams by now. You walk steadily as if this was your daily journey to work.

Simple, you are at home again! Here is the Market Square with its potholed pavement. You know all the houses; you look at them as a bookshop keeper may look at his shelves. All in their places, all with their meaning. You assure yourself that a new building down on the right is in the appropriate place, and you are satisfied as if you have built it there yourself. There is a new neon lighting advertisement over there, well, what can one say, the town is moving ahead.

All seems so peaceful! There are plenty of people everywhere. Trams and cars are making the same kind of noise as anywhere else in the world and yet the town seems calm, the noise quiet. You walk on, your step is accelerating. You are in your little street already. You stop automatically, you are at home.

Jizera Mountains
Two paintings by Ernest Gutmann

METHUSELAH

3 billion years ago until now

I am only a tiny, infinitesimal molecule, but I am infinitely important.

I am so very old! I emerged from the primeval soup as a little protein molecule some three billion years ago. At the very beginning, after the Big Bang, during all those fiery upheavals in which our planet Earth was created, it was too hot for my liking. I had to wait until that hot soup cooled down. To start with, my simpler and more resilient ancestor molecules prepared the ground for Life on Earth. A miracle! Given the right conditions, miracles can and do happen. And, as you all know, during those five billion years after the Big Bang, some lucky breaks did occur. My relatives had spread around the planet in many shapes and sizes because my kind of molecule was so badly needed for life. Now I can say with some pride that my descendants are dispersed all over the planet's living kingdom. I doubt that there is any living creature on Earth that can exist without at least one member of my numerous families. I am so ancient - some people call me Methuselah after the oldest, the longest-lived patriarch from the Bible.

What I mean is that life just couldn't exist without me! It's me and my progeny who give cells a shape. Cells are the building blocks of life. Bacteria make do with just one cell each, roundworms with a thousand or so, but the human body has some 37 trillion cells. They need support. Just imagine! Imagine what would you look like if you had no bones and no skeleton. You'd be an embarrassing blob, unable to move and thus unable to feed yourself, to multiply, to live. And the same goes for every single cell in your body. Would you want to be made of ungainly blobs? Certainly not. It's my descendants who keep you all in shape. They keep you on the go, they make you active. That's why most people call me Actin. Actin for Action.

Think of your muscles for example. Muscle cells are very active, and they couldn't be so without actin molecules. Not just muscle cells, all cells need to be active one way or another. And therefore, they need actin. There are so many of us actin molecules and our relatives! Some of your cells are nearly bursting with us. We move various bits and pieces from one end of a cell to another. In order to transport other molecules, organelles, or even whole cells, we pull, push, poke and squeeze, grasp and hold on. We also boss many other little molecules around to give us a hand with our innumerable tasks. In turn, we get orders from other cells, they send us various signals that control our activity. Yes, cells have their wicked ways to let us know when and where we are needed. Their wish is our command.

As time progressed, cells became more and more demanding, and we had to recruit an ever-greater variety of helper molecules to fulfil cellular demands. We used a trial-and-error approach and didn't expect any gratitude for all this hard work. We didn't grumble. In fact, we had and still have great fun with our collaborator molecules. With their assistance, we can assemble into all kinds of exciting shapes: filaments, nets, bundles, sheets, and even a wobbly jelly. Together we can form a sort of scaffolding that comes together or disbands as ordered. This cell scaffolding is called a cytoskeleton. We, the actin family, together with our collaborator molecules, are its proud members. Together we can pull, push, poke and squeeze even better. We have laboured quietly for billions of years, and nobody even knew about our existence.

Actin filament   *Actin monomer*

With time, cells grouped together to become ever more complicated beasts, of which humans are the most tiresome. Due to their voracious curiosity, humans meddle in everything. For three billion years we, the molecules of the cytoskeleton, have kept quiet, our chin down to the drawing board. But eventually, human meddlers found us out. Don't think we made it easy for them – it took them thousands of years to even get a hunch that we exist. Now, they are only just beginning to understand our games, still struggling with us while we play hide and seek with them.

Humans are very young, little infants eagerly discovering there is more to life than meets the eye. I, Methuselah, have seen it all. I and my progeny. We deserve to be left in peace. We don't need humans meddling with us. The tricks they come up with! They are pasting all sorts of coloured labels on us to make us glow and sparkle in the dark so that they can see us better. After they have stained us red or green or whatever, they take the cells out and put them into gigantic machines to take pictures of us. They are trying to find out where inside the cells we reside. Humans are checking on us in every cellular nook and cranny. Where is it going to end up? God only knows.

Still, let's be honest: who doesn't like a bit of adulation? We little cytoskeleton molecules, even though ancient and wise, feel rather thrilled, flattered, and uplifted to be finally seen and appreciated in all our beauty. And perhaps sometimes - on those rare occasions when we get out of kilter – not our fault I can assure you, it's down to those puffed-up genes who always think they know better – perhaps sometimes those irritating humans could be of some use and help us to get things right? God only knows.

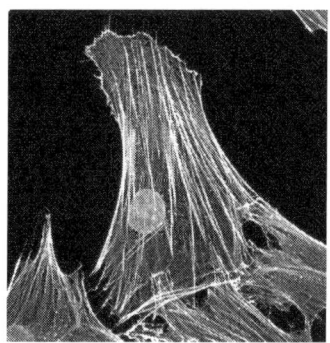

Actin filaments in fibroblast cells.

VISITING PROFESSOR KOHN
1952

"I will break this house to pieces!"

In our family, the story of my shouting has been told so many times over that I may well have incorporated it as my own memory. Apparently, I shouted because I was terribly bored; I had to sit, quiet and motionless, for my portrait to be painted by Mr Polívka. There was no way to get out of this: having their children's portrait painted was the height of fashion in those days. I was about six years old. I know this because my dress in the painting is the same as the one I wore in the school photograph, class 2A, with our teacher Comrade Michlová.

I don't have any clear recollections of Mr Polívka, the painter, but I do remember being bored and frustrated. In my mind, I see myself portrait-sitting in the apartment of old Professor Kohn. Why was I being painted in that place? I will never know. Perhaps the painter was the professor's friend? I sat unhappily while my father and the professor were enjoying a lively conversation. I didn't understand a word of it; they were speaking German. That's how I remember it: the old professor's flat packed with old furniture covered with lace runners. Professor Alfred Kohn was sitting in his study behind a desk and my father on a chair next to him. They seemed to be having a great time, laughing and beaming affectionately at each other. The professor's housekeeper, Anna, was always smiling. She brought them tea and a marble cake, and talked to me gently in Czech, encouraging me to be well-behaved. "Be patient, I have saved the best piece of cake for you," she promised. "Mr Polívka is nearly finished." The painter and I were in the room next to the study, but we could both see and hear the two men, cheerfully chatting over their tea. I could feel the deep respect and love that my father had for the old professor. The way he greeted him, the way he delighted in each of his words. The way smiling Anna walked around quietly checking that everything was as it should be, peaceful, amiable, protected and safe. She was not as old as the professor, but she could well be the fairy tale granny I had always wished for. The atmosphere was that of a fairy tale, in which a precious gem, a treasure of friendship, was guarded. If only I would have been allowed to walk around, observe, and help!

The memories of the visits to Professor Kohn are strong and genuine. They keep coming back. Who was he? Why did my father admire him so? I should have asked such questions earlier. Now I must try to find out what I can. Luckily, there are Runia's memoirs. Runia was a friend and a fellow medical student with my parents in Prague in the 1930s. She had written a lot about the professor, also with great admiration. Some twenty years ago, she gave me a copy of her memoirs. They were written in German. I have finally reached a stage when I can, with some help from a dictionary, pore over them.

In the early 1930s, Alfred Kohn, Professor of Histology at the Medical Faculty of the German University of Prague, was one of the most popular lecturers. When he taught, the halls were packed. His lectures were not only brilliant scientifically, but also full of erudite references to numerous literary works. The professor discovered and pioneered research on parathyroid glands, chromaffin cells and sympathetic paraganglia. In 1930, he was nominated for the Nobel Prize in physiology and medicine.

Professor Alfred Kohn in 1900s

After the Nazi occupation of Czechoslovakia in 1939, Professor Kohn, Jewish, then already 72 years old and retired, had to wear the notorious yellow star. Many of his fellow workers avoided him on the street. He was deported to the Theresienstadt Camp in 1943. Incredibly, he survived, being protected by two previous colleagues who had access to the camp. Although they became Nazis, they – paradoxically - remained Kohn's admirers. After the war, again incredibly, Professor Kohn was able to return to his very own Prague flat in Ječná Street. That was thanks to his faithful housekeeper, Anna, who had looked after him since 1912. She was thinking ahead and had changed the ownership of the flat from his name to hers. Because she was classified as an Aryan, she prevented its confiscation by the Nazis, a normal routine for the apartments of the deported Jews.

After the war, another confiscation of the flat in Ječná Street threatened. This was owing to Professor Kohn's pre-war position at the now abolished German University of Prague. The newly established post-war regime introduced strictly anti-German policies. Termination of the professor's superannuation money was imminent for the same reason. This time, another one of the professor's medical students and admirers put a word in for him, and the catastrophe was prevented. She was the wife of the communist Minister of Interior. And so, the professor and Anna continued to live peacefully in that same apartment.

Like Anna, the old professor was also thinking ahead. Being well over eighty, he wanted Anna's future to be financially secure and so he – the eternal bachelor - decided to marry her. He died in 1959, just short of 92 years old. But his faithful Anna, aged 69, could not face life without him. She committed suicide a few months after his death.

During my childhood visits to Ječná Street, I didn't know anything of the professor's story but I could feel the extraordinary atmosphere in that flat. Now, I understand that for my father it must have been like stepping back into the good old times of the pre-war First Republic. Back to a little piece of that past that had miraculously survived the most terrifying events and remained as it was then. Back to the language of his childhood: my father came from the Sudetenland and German was his first language. I remember the gusto with which he spoke it. Perhaps that is the reason why I always felt it was my duty to learn it. For my father, entering that same old flat to visit his favourite teacher must have been like stepping back to his happy student years. Yes, there were serious conflicts with some of the German students at the German University of Prague. But in the early 1930s, nobody could foresee where these skirmishes with the supporters of the pro-Hitler "Sudeten German Home Front" would lead. Besides, in Czechoslovakia in the fifties, he was also stepping away from the dreadful political situation of that time.

For me as a child, the strongest impression was that of seeing my father treating someone with such respect, care, and admiration. It was almost like an act of worship. Perhaps I shouted because I resented being constrained to the chair, being excluded from taking part, together with my father and Anna, in caring for that obviously very special person. Mr Polívka did his very best to make the portrait look angelic enough for my parents to be pleased with it. But when I look closer, I always remember my shouting.

Helena's portrait by Václav Polívka

Always Ready
1953 - 1962

1953

We stand proudly in our school assembly room, reciting the Pioneers' Oath. We are seven-year-old and all of us are wearing crisp white shirts and red scarves tied around our necks. Girls in blue skirts, boys in blue trousers. Saluting with our right arms, we solemnly declare that we shall always be ready to build and defend our socialist motherland. My chest is heaving with pride: I know that, with all my might, I must fight the enemies who threaten our country. Always ready. My head is full of stories about selfless heroic acts. We read them at school and watch films about them too. My favourite hero is Zoya Kosmodemyanskaya, the brave Soviet schoolgirl who became a partisan. She died a heroic death, fighting the Nazis. I want to be fearless like her.

My sister Sandra is eleven, old enough to make good use of my obsession. She suggests we play; she'll be a Nazi and I'll be Zoya Kosmodemyanskaya. She pushes me onto the sofa, grabs my arm, and twists it behind my back.

"Why did you burn our houses? Who helped you? Where are they hiding?" Sandra, the Nazi, shouts.

"I was alone," I insist. "Nobody helped me!" It hurts, but I repeat defiantly, "I was on my own." Because I must never betray my fellow partisans.

It's April 1953 and what had happened just a month ago adds to the gravity of the situation. Within a couple of weeks, both Stalin, the Soviet leader, and Gottwald, the Czechoslovak president, had died. Solemn and tearful speeches poured out of the radio and our parents listened with worried expressions. Obviously, something terrible and very serious was going on Radio broadcasts of funereal music lasted for a week or so and anxiety ruled our home. Finally, the funereal marches were replaced by cheerful folk songs: we got a new president, Antonín Zápotocký.

Zoya's struggle must go on. I look resolutely into Sandra's eyes. "You can do whatever you like, I have nothing to say!"
"You must die!" Sandra proclaims and leads me to the gallows.

1956

We are sitting at our school benches, textbooks neatly piled on the left side of the desks. Our teacher, Comrade Šebestová, is handing out scissors and black marker pens.

"Open your Math Book on page three and cut that page out," she says. Page three is a glorified portrait of our late Great Leader Comrade Joseph Vissarionovich Stalin. Page four with Lenin's portrait stays put, but page five with Comrade Klement Gottwald goes out too.

"Now open your Czech Grammar Book. Cut out pages three and five." All our textbooks contain Stalin's and Gottwald's portraits, so we accumulate quite a collection of them. Comrade Šebestová continues: "Find page 24 and with your black markers cross out 'Stalin, the Bright Falcon.' Yes, black out the whole poem."

She pauses awkwardly and then offers. "As Comrade Nikita Khrushchev said, we had worshipped certain leaders far too much. This is called the Cult of Personality and it's wrong. We learn from our mistakes, don't we? So, we are doing this to correct our errors, to overcome the Cult of Personality."

These 'corrections' take over all of our math class. At the end, Comrade Šebestová walks between the benches, collecting the cut-out pages into a large canvas bag.

After the lesson Venda beckons to me, he wants to show me something. He is my unlikely friend. Unlikely because he is the naughtiest boy in the class, and I am the goodie goodie. However, we share a passion for Jules Verne's books. He likes me because I have lent him 'Twenty Thousand Leagues Under the Sea' and I like him because he is the one I can talk to about these books. He also lent me 'Journey to the Centre of the Earth' and a rare copy of the 'Children of Captain Grant.'

Discreetly, Venda pulls out an assortment of torn-out pages from his school bag. Stalin has got a mustache here, a clown's hat there, red hot lips here, a turban there. Gottwald received a black tooth on one page, funny glasses or a dripping nose and donkey's ears on other pages. We both burst out laughing but then stop suddenly. Comrade Šebestová is approaching, frowning and disapproving.

"What have you got there?"

Quickly, Venda shoves the papers back and with "Sorry, I am really desperate," he disappears into the boys' lavatories.

"What did you laugh about?" the teacher asks, and I am ready, always ready.

"Oh, he muddled his homework so badly, we had to laugh."

1959

I am nearly fourteen and ready to see the sights. Dana is my best friend. We like to wander around and explore the city. We creep into old courtyards with their balconies, called 'pavlače'. They overlook the falling masonry and gloom. We breathe in the mixture of humidity and the sick acid smell of urine. There is also a whiff of roses and perhaps jasmine. But the main smell is that of baking and cooking, onions being fried everywhere. We spy on the secret lives behind the curtained windows. Sometimes we get told off, but we are always ready with an answer.

"What are you after? You don't live here."

"We are looking for Mr Zelenka," we say innocently. "Do you know him? He should be on the second floor."

"Never heard of him, not here."

"Oh sorry, it must be next door then." We retreat, chat about our discoveries and move on.

Dana and I live near Letná Park which sits on top of a hill with great views of Prague. We have learned to recognize some of the numerous church spires and bridges across the river. We point them out and test each other. At the very top of Letná, we can't avoid the ridiculously gigantic statue of Stalin. It still dominates the city, despite the efforts to correct our errors. A remnant of the Cult of Personality is too vast to be removed discreetly. This most enormous Stalin is followed by just as enormous a line of proud workers, farmers, and soldiers, ready to build and defend. The line is commonly known as a 'Meat Queue' since it reminds people of their eternal queueing for scarce produce. Its size makes us feel tiny and feeble: we play a game of 'Little Imbeciles'. We run around the statue and jump up and down the massive stairs, bending down to make us even smaller, frantically shaking our hands because we are imbeciles. It's summer, it's raining, it's pouring. We can smell the earth and the damp grass. We laugh hysterically, looking down at the red imprints that our wet shoelaces had made on our white socks.

The 'Meat Queue' – The outsize statue of Stalin

1962

On my way to school, a lorry carrying a large round object is passing by. As it approaches, I can see the familiar stone head. It's only partially covered. There is no mistake: some two meters in height - who's else can it be but Stalin's? I rush to tell all my schoolmates. Can it be true? In the afternoon, Dana and I go to check things out. We take a tram to Čechův most, the bridge just beneath the Letná Hill, and look up. Indeed, Stalin and his 'Meat Queue' are gone, demolished, blasted to smithereens. On the bridge, the graceful angels are still standing on the tall columns, solemnly and victoriously raising their sprigs high above the crowds milling down below. Wow! Dana and I look at each other and laugh. Laughter comes easy to us, almost as an instinct, an automatic response to our confusion. We climb the steps, but the access to the remnants of the statue is barricaded. We laugh yet again. We laugh at the news, since we don't believe any of it, we laugh at the boys making their awkward advances, we laugh at our teachers when they get into a pickle trying to explain ideas they themselves don't believe.

It's quite late by the time I get home. My parents are already there and, of course, I tell them about the demolition straight away. What do they think about it, ha? To my surprise, my father gets angry about my sarcastic tone.

"You are always ready to be critical and negative about everything. Why don't you get involved in something constructive?"

"How?" I defend myself. "With whom? Only careerists get involved nowadays. We can only wait and see how they'll muddle on. It's not our fault!"

"This is sad," my father looks crestfallen. "Young people are so disengaged. Not what we were like. Not what we had expected."

I try to soften the blow. "Nobody likes this disengagement, but what can we do? We are just waiting. Waiting for signs that something can be done."

"To whom can they look up to, Malka?" Father asks Mum now. "Do you think it's our failure?" He sounds exasperated. "It's a failure, isn't it, Malka?"

Sandra, David and I look at our Mum expectantly, but she just sighs and starts serving dinner. "I don't know, Ernest. We had such high hopes, high ideas. Perhaps things will get better, who knows? Let's get on with the dinner before it gets cold."

Stalin's statue demolished

ELISA'S LONELINESS
1960 – 1991 – 1995

Uncle Sunay's funeral in March 1991 was a strange affair. Auntie Elisa seemed not quite there, her face was blank and expressionless as I have always known it. I could never guess what was hiding behind that façade of hers. Auntie Elisa was my father's cousin. She left Prague for London in the thirties to escape the Nazis. There she met and married an Indian doctor, Uncle Sunay.

I haven't seen their daughter Anasuya for a long time. She was once a gorgeous beauty, so I was surprised to see how tired she looked now. In contrast, Anasuya's daughter was a picture of life itself; sporting a black tight décolleté dress, her skin glowing, a few weeks old baby on her arm. 'Blood and Milk' as my Mum would say. Anasuya's brother Raman had arrived from the US where he now works as a doctor. He came just for the funeral, he said, because he is busy at home and time is very precious. Still, we had lunch together afterwards, since he wanted to talk, to tell me that his childhood was very unhappy. "I know that everybody says so," he said, "but mine was very very very unhappy".

The first time I met Auntie Elisa's family was on a summer day in the early sixties. Uncle Sunay and Auntie Elisa arrived from London in Prague with their two teenage children. It was the time of "the thaw" in the Cold War when such travels became possible, and generally, there was more contact with the West. All of us were completely struck by Anasuya's exotic beauty. Petite and willowy, dark eyes, olive skin, dark shiny hair flowing over her shoulders.

What an unusual sight in our austere Czechoslovakia! She wore flowery short dresses or bright blouses with red shorts. Raman had tight-fitting jeans and his shirts were crisp and clean. People stared. I was so proud. It was a privilege to show this glamorous princess and her retinue around Prague.

One of the Prague sights was the four-hundred-year-old Pinkas Synagogue. After its recent restoration, the walls of the synagogue were covered with the names of some 79000 Czech and Moravian Jews murdered in the Holocaust. Auntie Elisa found the names of her parents, uncles, aunts and cousins. She burst into tears and couldn't stop sobbing. Uncle Sunay became very uncomfortable with this emotional outpouring. He stared at her from behind his dark-framed glasses, out of his immaculate suit, out of his white shirt with a bow tie, embarrassed and disapproving. The patriarch, whose rules must be obeyed.

"For goodness' sake, stop it!" he admonished her. "Control yourself, please!"

"Dad!" Anasuya exclaimed, her face flushed red. She was quite obviously shocked by and ashamed of her father's behaviour. She looked at Raman who just stared at the floor and didn't dare to say a word. Then she looked at me and my parents as if to say 'Please do something!'

There was an awkward silence except for Uncle Sunay's tut-tutting until finally, my father said "It's all right, Sunay, let her be, let her have her cry," and slowly we moved on to look at the ancient Jewish graves in the Old Cemetery. Never before had Anasuya seen her mother crying, as I have learned later.

After Uncle Sunay's funeral, Auntie Elisa deteriorated rapidly. When I visited her in the apartment, to which she and Sunay moved in their old age, I often found her deeply depressed, confused and gloomy. There were, however, occasional bursts of vivacity when her repressed personality seemed suddenly to emerge from the depths. She had an old friend called Traute, whose father was Franz Kafka's cousin. I met them both at dinner one evening.

"Oh, Kafka's cousin, was he?" I asked her. "So what does it mean to you?"

"Nothing," she said, "except that people go 'Oh, Ah, Oh'!"

The two old ladies looked at each other and started to giggle hysterically as if they had a special secret between them that nobody else could understand.

Another such outburst occurred during another visit to that sad apartment. As usual, Auntie Elisa walked around the room in circles, never sitting down, asking the customary automatic questions about the children and the family without any real interest.

"We are going to Šumava this winter," I told her, desperately trying to enliven our conversation, "Böhmerwald, you know?"

"Oh yes!" she said, and her face brightened. She started to sing, swaying her body from side to side: "Tief drin im Böhmerwald, da liegt mein Heimatort; es ist gar lang schon her, dass ich von dort bin fort....." There deep in Böhmerwald lies my homeland, I left it so long ago.....

Elisa came from Sudetenland and her first language was German, just like my father's. Her eyes half closed, she continued to sing and even started to waltz. "Es war im Böhmerwald, wo meine Wiege stand...." It was there, in the beautiful green Bohemian Forest where my cradle stood.

"Wow, Elisa, how wonderful! You can still remember the song!"

She stopped singing. "I was a student in Böhmerwald," she said. "Doing an apprenticeship to become a dental technician. But then I had to leave the country and here I am." The façade came back on again as if a ghost of disapproving Sunay wagged its finger at her.

Auntie Elisa survived Uncle Sunay for four years only. Another funeral, another family gathering. Meeting my cousins again. Wondering – how do they feel? What was it like for Anasuya and Raman to live with one peremptory parent demanding absolute obedience in an old-fashioned Indian style and the other submissive, but still expecting perfect middle-European manners? On the outside, however, both were more English than English. It must have been difficult. Very very very difficult.

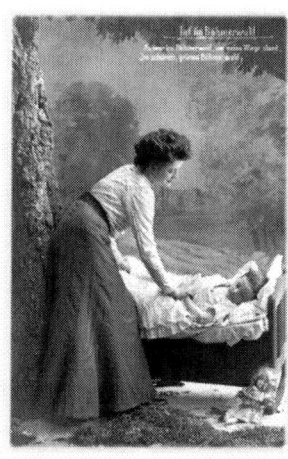

Tief drin im Böhmerwald

POSH CARS
1961 - 2012

The American film animator Gene Deitch was famous for his collaboration on the Popeye and Tom and Jerry series, as well as for his very unusual life as "the only free American living and working in Prague during 30 years of the Communist Party dictatorship". He died in April 2020, aged 95, in the middle (but not because) of the Corona crisis. A friend of mine sent me a book of his memoirs, "For the love of Prague." What a perfect read for the lockdown!

Deitch's description of Prague in the 60s is not quite as I remember it. His American eyes saw the shortages and the shabbiness, and his American taste buds were nauseated by dumplings and pork knuckles. In contrast, my memories are tinted by the sweetness of childhood and youth, which even the dullest apparatchiks could not sully. But I forgive him because, however critical, his love of Prague permeates all the pages.

The book has a chapter called 'The Great White Saab.' It describes Deitch's friendship with Mr T, a racing car driver who, through some efficient wheeling and dealing, managed to procure a white Saab not only for his American friend but for himself too. Reading this chapter was a delight since I knew Mr T, his wife, and his children very well. Their cottage in the mountains was not far from ours. Mrs T was a very graceful and cultured woman, a music teacher. I felt so sorry for her when, in that same chapter, Gene Deitch relates how he refused to eat her welcome offering, a slice of rye bread with goose fat, an exquisite delicacy, usually served with chopped goose liver. He couldn't eat that gunk, he says! I imagined Mrs T smiling charmingly and serving him a hot dog instead.

Occasionally, the very same Mr T would invite us, eager teenagers, into his illustrious white Saab and give us a ride along the meandering mountain lanes. Down into the village, perhaps stopping in front of a shop to allow people to gather around and stare while we nonchalantly paid for our groceries. They stared because a white Saab was an absolute sensation among battered Škodas and Trabants of Czechoslovakia, and doubly so in those remote mountains. Mr T was a busy man, so such treats were rare, but we were able to expand the pleasure by playing a 'How we ride the Saab' game. You let your right hand hang all limp to show it's not made for any work, with your left hand you wave to the masses, and you look down your nose as you command whoever the chauffeur is to speed up or slow down.

The white Saab story triggered another memory, an episode that occurred some fifty years later. My then-boyfriend got himself a new BMW and was eager to show me his magnificent new toy. We were speeding along the M4 towards Monmouthshire, our first weekend away. All he could talk about was his BMW. How it can park itself, look - no hands, how it bleeps to warn you that there are speed cameras around, how you can see your speed glowing in red letters on the windscreen. And so nifty, look, he stepped on it, it accelerates to 90 miles per hour just like that. I feared for my life and all I wished for was for him to slow down. He must have been frustrated with my lack of appreciation.

By then, after half a century of having lived in the 'West' and having been flooded with endless contraptions, my appetite for marvels of technology had subsided. The unqualified admiration we used to have for new gadgets had gone. What impresses now are things simple and functional, unfussy and durable, cars solid, somewhat weathered and understated. In the days of Mr T's Saab, we craved forbidden fruit from exotic capitalist El Dorado countries. Chewing gum, fine wool jumpers, nylon raincoats, tape recorders, LPs, jeans, especially jeans. In the sixties, my father had finally been allowed to travel to England, and he finally brought me a pair of craved-for jeans. They had a zip at the front! At the time, I considered that unacceptable, unladylike. So, I spent all my pocket money on having the zip's position changed to the side.

On the way to Monmouthshire, sitting in the posh car driven by my boyfriend, I kept reminding myself that I must be understanding: for him, driving his new BMW is very exciting. But still, I would have felt better if at least a smidgeon of that excitement was directed at me.

Things got better after dinner. I couldn't doubt his enthusiasm in bed, and felt reassured. But then again, things got much worse. The next day we went for a hike, and my then-boyfriend walked half a mile ahead of me. Though he waited for me occasionally to catch up with him, his attention was focused entirely on miles covered and those to be covered yet. There was hardly any other conversation. It was more like a military expedition than a romantic weekend away.

He got very upset with the way I wore my anorak, sleeves just tied up around my shoulders so I wouldn't get too hot when climbing. The wind could blow it away, he said, and he wasn't going to run down the slope to save it for me. It must be his mariner background, I thought. He had spent some years in the navy and got used to giving and taking orders. I stood my ground. Nobody is going to order me how to wear my anorak!

I don't know how I survived the following day in Monmouthshire, balancing between tolerance, acceptance, resignation and outrage. While driving back in the posh BMW, feverish thoughts of 'Should I go, or should I stay?' pounded inside my head. My automatic reaction always was to search for my own wrongdoings. Wishful thinking was another factor. I was in my sixties, perhaps this was my last chance. After three further turbulent months, we parted. I sincerely hope that he has eventually found a partner who is a better match for him and his new BMW.

Mr T, the racing driver of exotic cars, died aged 70 in a car accident, just four years before the 'Velvet Revolution' which ended the 41 years of the socialist era in Czechoslovakia. Gene Deitch's account of those heady historic days in November 1989 and the events that followed was written right there and then with great enthusiasm and hope. "Well," he says in mid 1990s, "the air is bustling with change – some good, some doubtful, some quite bad. Time will tell, but we still think it was well worth it." And ten years later: "Greed, corruption, criminality, and growing tawdriness have brought home to us the bitter fact that however we fantasised, this is just an ordinary country after all. But yet I still feel it's better than most."

The country is full of posh cars now and nobody stares at them anymore. I look back with some nostalgia at the times when we were riding the white Saab full of pride and with a simple faith in those new machines and contraptions that would sort all our problems.

White Saab sensation in socialist Czechoslovakia

DAVID'S STORY
Based on his letters 1968 - 1977

In the summer of 1968, my brother David found himself stranded in Israel, confused, and wondering what to do with himself. He was only 19 years old and had left Czechoslovakia for a short exploratory trip to Israel. While he was there, Czechoslovakia was invaded by the Soviets, providing a 'brotherly help to suppress a counter-revolution,' thus ending the exciting days of the Prague Spring.

It was not the first time that my brother was stranded in the great wide world. The previous year, shortly before his final High School exams were due, he had escaped to Bulgaria. While there, he had shepherded sheep in the mountains and thought things over. To the great relief of our family and friends, he had returned just in time to pass his exams. He then enrolled to study Chinese at Prague University.

Now that he found himself outside the Iron Curtain, he could suddenly go anywhere he wanted. Should he go back home regardless of the grim developments there? Our parents understood that things were likely to go badly and did not insist on his return. David was full of conflicting desires. On one side there were his parents' expectations that he should study, the expectations that he internalised; on the other there was his longing to be free, unburdened, have fun, travel. Whatever he did, he missed his family and his beleaguered country intensely.

Thanks to the encouragement and help from his parents, he got a grant to study Chinese in Cambridge. It seemed a magnificent opportunity; David had been fascinated by the Far East since childhood. Moreover, my then-husband Paul and I had already emigrated to England and lived in London.

In the late autumn of 1968, David arrived at Cambridge and tried to mingle with the local academia. It didn't work. He soon took an active dislike to that environment. Too restrained, too pompous, formal, no fun. He felt straitjacket restrained and sought release. He used to visit us in London, often bringing an assortment of jolly guests. To celebrate our first New Year's Eve in emigration, he brought a drunken Irishman who had promptly consumed all the available alcohol before he continued his New Year celebrations elsewhere. Back in Cambridge, David didn't feel inspired to work hard and didn't get on with his tutors. The dislike was mutual; his tutors, in turn, considered him to be a "wasted investment". That was the last straw. "I am not an investment!" he raged. In the summer of 1969, David went back to Israel.

He felt much better among the informal mishmash of the many nationalities that he encountered; first in a kibbutz, where he was working and learning Hebrew, and later at Jerusalem University. He got a small grant to study Chinese and Russian Literature. This time he did work hard. He loved the languages and read Russian books. He made many friends and enjoyed the support and the company of his Israeli aunt, uncle, and cousins. Still, there was financial insecurity and uncertainty. His plans kept changing from one day to another. He wanted to travel to China, Japan, India, France, Iran. He added more languages to those that he already studied: Japanese, Hindi, French and Persian filled his free time.

But he still missed his parents, felt guilty for leaving them behind, and was sad, nostalgic, and heartbroken about the separation brought about by the nonsensical politics. He expressed these thoughts in many letters that he wrote to our parents. Should he just go back home?

Israel had a lot to offer. People whose history was shocking, but also so familiar. There was no need to explain who you were, they knew. David felt the attraction, perhaps almost the call of the blood as he roamed the green hills with their olive groves or as he stared at the desolate moonscape of the Negev desert. He was imagining himself as one of those thirsty, wailing wandering Jews, roaming through the desert, looking for a home. At one stage, he even contemplated whether he should become a rabbi. An academic career was an option too. He did well at the university and enjoyed much greater academic freedom than he had had at Cambridge. Should he stay in Israel?

There were two big problems with that. Firstly, accepting Israeli citizenship would have meant **ruling out** his way home completely because of the current political situation. Secondly, he could never envisage himself spending three years in the army, unavoidable since conscientious objections were unacceptable. The only route to avoid the army would have been to become ultra-orthodox. That was out of the question.

If David ever felt any rabbinic calling, that was soon dispelled by his experiences with the orthodox Jews. The following episode was the last straw. One Sabbath evening, David was enjoying dinner with his friend, who was a doctor. A telephone call from the doctor's father interrupted them. The father was taken ill and asked his son to come and see him urgently. David knew the old man well, a lovable Austro-Hungarian charmer, polite but acerbic, erudite but self-effacing. He would never make a fuss for no reason. The two friends set out immediately. The journey from Beer Sheva to Jerusalem is about a 90-minute drive. They were nearly at their destination when they heard a terrible racket: stones, thrown from the bridge above, were ricocheting off the car roof. One of them shattered the front screen and narrowly missed the driver. "Bloody Frums!" he yelled, quite shaken. "The ultra-orthodox," he explained. David wanted to chase after them, but there was no point, they were gone already. The main thing was to help the doctor's father as soon as possible, which is what they did.

David finished his BA degree successfully both in Russian and Chinese. With the Israeli options closed to him, he left for England in 1973, shortly before the Yom Kippur War started. He stayed there with us; he arrived soon after we had become parents to our first-born son Matthew. David was assessing his chances. He wanted to continue with his Russian studies, but it would have been too expensive in England. Living and studying in France was cheaper.

David left for Paris in the autumn of 1974. Despite his totally impractical character, he survived and succeeded in completing his Russian and Chinese degrees at the Sorbonne. He lived on next to nothing and constantly worried about the numerous documents he needed to justify his existence. Occasional packages from our parents in Prague contained trousers and jackets that were mostly too big for him. They made him smile and ache for home. Yet, he made many friends and travelled extensively. He continued visiting me in London, often bringing his friends along. A beautiful French girl with long skirts and long hair, a charming shiny-eyed man, high on marijuana and continuously ecstatic, especially when taken to walk the Welsh hills. These exotic people and David's bohemian image, his full beard, and a halo of unruly curly hair, brought some thrill to my rather quiet suburban life.

David's next move was to Berlin. There was a good chance for him to obtain German citizenship and a passport on account of his father's history: German schools and the German University of Prague. It was a long process, but David badly needed a document to travel with, to prove **he was a person that belonged somewhere, that exists**. While waiting, he was learning German at the Goethe Institute and making numerous contradictory plans: to work on his Ph.D.in Berlin, to travel to the Far East, to go back to France. He didn't take to the German **language easily**, perhaps because he was obliged to learn it; he did not choose it. Again, he managed to get a small grant to work on his thesis: "Buddhist – Confucian Syncretism and its Significance at the End of the Chinese Dynasties." To earn a little extra and save up for his future travels, he worked as a night porter at a Psychiatric Clinic. They were not happy times. The thought that he was now so close to Prague - just a few hours by train - but could not go there, made him "incurably anxious". He took his father's advice to heart and started running to improve his mental and physical state.

David collected the materials for his thesis but felt that the Berlin environment was not ideal for his subject. He couldn't gather much enthusiasm for it. Japanese was his side subject, pursued with much greater fervour. With that, he had plenty of help from his new girlfriend Michiko. The Eastern Pull was growing stronger and stronger. David was visiting the Buddhist Temple in Berlin / Frohnau, practicing yoga and meditation, and making friends at the Temple. As soon as he had received his German passport, he was off to India. "Don't worry," he wrote to our parents, "I have a return ticket." He stayed there for nearly six months, blissfully happy to finally realise his childhood dreams.

David came back to Berlin in May 1977 and moved in with Michiko. He reluctantly continued with his thesis and wondered if he would ever finish it. He dreamt about his next journeys to the East. As the summer approached, there came exciting news: our parents were finally both allowed to visit London to meet the family and their two little grandsons, 4 and 2 years old. That was very rare; usually, one of the pair had to stay behind as a sort of hostage. Plans were made immediately for a great reunion in London. We collected Mum and Dad from Heathrow airport and there followed a week of intense and very emotional catching up, trying to squeeze the nine years of missed contact into that short time. David went running with Dad each morning and then they sat talking for hours.

Then came a terrible shock. One day, I drove Mum and Dad to Cambridge to visit Dad's scientific colleague; David and Paul stayed at home with the children. On our way home, our father suddenly died of a heart attack caused by coronary thrombosis. Our broken family had to deal with the unexpected blow, each of us in our own way. When David returned to Berlin, he cried and cried and there was nothing Michiko could do to comfort him.

David married Michiko and their daughter Izumi was born in 1984. His happiness intermingled with increasingly frequent attacks of great turmoil and misery. He was spending more and more time at the Frohnau Buddhist Temple, trying to find some peace and stability, away from the complexities of his relationship and his material worries. The work on his doctorate was half-hearted, perhaps he stopped believing in its usefulness. Perhaps the gap left by our father's absence had something to do with it. He couldn't take our mother's encouragements quite as seriously as those of our father's. Her ideas about "active rest" and her unshakeable work ethic seemed to him, from the Buddhist point of view, more like distracted unrest. In their letters, it was now he who was advising her on how to calm down.

David never finished his Ph.D. on the Buddhist – Confucian Syncretism although he had spent nearly ten years working at it. In 1986, he made a life-changing decision and departed for Sri Lanka. David had left all his obligations behind and eventually emerged, ordained and transformed into the Venerable Dharmakara. But that's another story.

Ordained and transformed

TWO TEENAGERS AND BIG MAMA

1988

Holidays! And what should a newly divorced single mother do to entertain her two teenage sons? Matthew and Oliver had recently acquired bicycles and had shown keen interest, so how about cycling in Ireland? So far, in the 42 years of my life, I have cycled about five miles altogether. Would I be able to do this? And what about the boys? Was it pushing them too far? I got plenty of good advice and encouragement from a tall Dutch postdoc in the lab, an experienced cyclist. What kind of bike should I get? What panniers, racks, lights, helmets, what are the essentials for a three-week tour? I studied maps and read eagerly about the Emerald Isle and the plan took shape: Ferry from Swansea to Cork, one week of cycling, one restful week on the Sheep Peninsula, and another week of cycling around Killarney. And then back to Cork.

The Swansea to Cork overnight ferry, the Celtic Pride, was run by a Polish crew. A free sauna was available on board, which helped to instill that relaxed holiday feeling. However, after we had landed at Ringaskiddy Port, we were thrown straight into the deep end. To get to Kinsale, where our first youth hostel was booked, we had to cycle some 35 miles in pouring rain. Of course, the teenagers protested, but Big Mama – as they now called me – decided to push on. Our afflictions were dutifully recorded, joint efforts, in our travel diary:

In our summery mood and summery clothes, we freewheeled excitedly from the ship, greeting Ireland with a friendly 'Hello!'

'Bugger off,' it yelled back at us, brewing up a fine concoction of mud, water, and grit, to sling at our faces.

We still pretended heroically that it was summer, it was our holiday, and we were going to have a jolly good time.

Matthew was desperate for McDonald's, so we diverted to Cork Centre. Our utter despair was alleviated by a stop at a friendly café which provided beefburgers for the boys (close enough to those from McDonald's) and a hot apple pie with cream for Big Mama. Fortunately, the café radio announced, just in time, that parents are the ultimate authority, so – grabbing the chance while Matthew was subdued by the burgers – Big Mama decided that we'd leave Cork immediately and cycle to Kinsale. Come hell or high water….

Torrential downpour and twenty miles to go, we wondered: should we have stayed in Cork? NO! said Big Mama. The rain seemed to have affected her usual intelligence.

There wasn't a single dry fibre left on our bodies when by 2 pm we finally arrived at Kinsale (by a route that should have been scenic had we been able to see anything through the rain).

After this alarming start, our holiday turned out to be a great adventure, one of my proudest achievements. I can only hope that the boys liked it too, although there were some tough days, especially for Oliver, who was then only 13 years old. Matthew, at 15, was already quite strong and knowledgeable about bikes. He could even mend punctures! That was a blessing. And Ireland was a blessing too. Cruising on little country lanes along the southwest coast, the sea all around, green rolling hills, fuchsia hedges, little fjords, the air moist and warm, people friendly, interested, and happy to philosophise. The weather was hardly ever mentioned. Instead, there was 'Where do you hail from? What do you think of this or that? Ready to engage with you in sorting the world out at any time.

Matthew and Oliver at the Gap of Dunloe

The best thing was the sharing of experiences with my two wonderful sons; pride and joy swelling in my chest each time I looked at them. We drifted along, discovering yet another amazing coastal vista and stopping there for a wonderful picnic, or we took a break at some remote café only to be surprised by exceptionally good food. What we ate was always carefully recorded in our travel journals. The restful week at a rented cottage on the Sheep Peninsula afforded particularly noteworthy culinary occasions. Our neighbour was a kind elderly Russian called Mr. Gogol who loved going fishing. Every morning he visited us with his catch and asked, "Do you vont any fish?" And so, we enjoyed a week of delicious fresh mackerels, lightly grilled and sprinkled with lemon, which helped greatly to recharge our batteries while leisurely exploring that beautiful remote headland.

Helena at Allihies, Beara Peninsula

The bad episodes were recorded too: Matthew's camera was stolen, and Oliver suffered a terrible headache one day:

Matthew: *Gits, gits, gits, I could easily dismember them with two oversized toothpicks and a red-hot poker. Anger, anger, anger. Anyway, on with the story.*

Oliver: *My head is pulsing and making my brain stretch and contract! I feel like it will burst. Ahhh!*

There was one other day, cycling to Bantry, when we got completely soaked. But how lucky we were there with our B&B! The landlady not only washed and dried our clothes, but she also drove us to 'Peter's Grill', a restaurant she highly recommended. That too was duly recorded: *Story of a Good Woman*.

The holiday was a success. In the two following summers, we repeated the idea and cycled around in Devon and Wales. Afterward, the teenagers liked to go on their own cycle tours with their friends. That, I thought, was also a success. And eventually, I found a group of cycling enthusiasts, who tolerated my slow pace and my penchant for tea rooms stops. I have enjoyed many more cycling holidays with them.

MUSCLE CONTRACTIONS
1993

My colleague Muriel had a strong sense of duty and took all her obligations very seriously. She was responsible for the first-year students' practical classes on Human Muscle Contraction. To make sure everything worked just fine, she asked all the helpers and demonstrators to come to the class at least an hour before the start. I already knew the practical backwards and forwards, had done it a hundred times, but how could I refuse Muriel? We agreed to have lunch together before the class.

"Hi Helena, it's time to go!" She barged into my lab to summon me. "Remember we have to be in the class early!"

***

We got to know each other gradually over occasional lunches. We were both senior lecturers in our late forties, both divorced, both struggling with work and with men. Muriel was going through a difficult patch on both fronts.

She was a slim and pretty woman. If she had wanted, she could have looked spectacular, but her style was understated. She never wore any makeup, and her clothes were stern and somewhat mousy. In fact, she reminded me of a Victorian governess. In spite of this, or perhaps because of it, she had attracted the attention of a single-minded professor, a tall, bird-like man, from one of the neighbouring departments. His determination and drive were universally known and admired as well as feared. His private life, however, was chaotic. Last summer, he seemed to be right in the middle of a severe midlife crisis and pursued Muriel relentlessly.

To start with, she resisted his advances.

"I don't want to get involved in his mess," she told me resolutely at that time. "Before chasing anybody else, he should be sorting his own marriage out. He doesn't know where he's going or what he wants."

"You know he has a reputation of being quite ruthless, don't you?" I warned her. "Speak to any of his postdocs."

"I know," Muriel sighed. "But he's fun to be with, I must admit. And I don't know that many intelligent and witty men."

"You two are very different, aren't you?"

"Yes, that's true. He loves the limelight, goes to parties and society dinners. And I? I like beavering quietly in the lab and wandering in the country in my free time."

"He likes power. He gets involved in all kinds of management issues. But – who knows - perhaps it could work out well. They say opposites attract. I should keep my mouth shut."

"No, don't," Muriel said quickly. "You have a point. Perhaps it's my Mother Teresa nature. Perhaps I think I can show him the way like Dante's Beatrice. He seems so lost and confused."

"Be careful!" I warned her again. "Perhaps he just needs an escape from his domestic upheavals."

"Perhaps," she half-agreed. "That's why I don't want to get involved. I don't want students and colleagues to see us together. You know how people gossip. But he likes us to be seen together and bullies me about it."

"What do you mean?"

"He says I'm inhibited and need to see a psychotherapist!" Muriel laughed, but I didn't think it was funny.

***

That was about three months ago, and we hadn't lunched together since then. This time, Muriel looked faded and tearful, just like the autumn weather outside. Without any introduction, she went straight to the point.

"Well, he got me where he wanted, but he still doesn't know where he's going." She paused and looked at me unhappily. "Please don't say I told you so."

"I won't, don't worry. What's happening now?"

"What's happening now?" she repeated after me. "Now he wants me to go with him to a conference in California. Right now, leaving in three days. I don't know what to do. He says we'd stay there for two weeks, and he'd pay for everything."

"You don't sound so happy about that. Can you take that time off?"

"If I juggled things, I could. But I have a grant application deadline. My postdoc is leaving next month, we need to finish our paper. There is so much to do."

"Do you want to go?"

"Part of me wants to, but now is the worst possible time to go away." Muriel was in tears now. "What a mess!"

"Are you two at least having good times together?" I wondered.

"Yes and no, there is a thrill, but no calm, no way. Sometimes he's needy and loving, sometimes condescending and distant. Always self-deprecating and turning everything into a joke, but you never know what he's really thinking. Like a relationship with a kite."

"He's putting a lot of pressure on you."

"Yes. It's unsettling."

"I don't think that's right. It worries me. I wonder if he just can't bear to appear there on his own. The conference, various social functions, colleagues with their accompanying spouses, and there he is … without any … "

"He says he doesn't want to go alone, he'd feel terrible, he needs support."

"But so do you, Muriel, can't you see? Do you want to go?" I asked her again.

"Not really, not now. It would cause many problems at work."

"Well, don't go, he must understand that."

"I really can't afford to leave now," Muriel muttered more to herself than to me. "I am not going and that's it." She wiped her face, blew her nose and smiled. "I won't go, you are quite right, thanks.".

And we walked together to get the class organised.

At the class, I was ready for action, standing side by side with the other demonstrators and facing the students. Muriel was describing the method and the aim of the practical. She was quite composed and cool now, talking to the students cheerfully, slowly, and clearly.

"Today we are going to investigate how the strength of a skeletal muscle twitch varies with increasing stimulus strength." She pointed at me. "This is Helena, my colleague. She'll now apply some jelly to the electrode. She'll then strap the electrode, the anode, to my left wrist."

To show these objects to the students, I lifted the pot of jelly and the electrode up and, with a dramatic gesture, fastened the latter to Muriel's wrist.

"Now we will use a second electrode, the cathode," Muriel explained. "Here it is. A small pad soaked in a salt solution and connected to a stimulator." She passed the electrode to me. "Helena will use it to stimulate my *ulnar nerve*," she pointed to her wrist. "It may feel strange at first, like a gentle tingling on your skin, but it doesn't hurt."

Students looked on, horrified. "It can't do you any harm," Muriel added reassuringly.

I switched the stimulator on and started to explore Muriel's wrist with the salt pad to find the best position for stimulating the thumb muscle. Soon I had the right place. When I pressed the salt pad there, Muriel's thumb started to twitch vigorously. She was delighted, her worries momentarily forgotten. Here, in this rational, lucid, and manageable world she was safe.

"Look!" she beamed at the students. "Helena is applying electrical pulses to my *ulnar nerve*, which in turn stimulates the *adductor pollicis* muscle. Now we shall be recording my thumb's twitches. You will see how they increase in size with increasing stimulus strength."

To record the twitches, I secured Muriel's thumb in a Perspex frame connected to the recorder. I played with a stimulator, gradually increasing the voltage. Muriel's thumb responded beautifully. We recorded two twitches at each voltage. The thumb continued to twitch more and more forcefully, causing panic among students. Finally, the strength of the twitches had reached a plateau.

"Increase the voltage!", Muriel demanded. "More, more!" The students looked very worried now, but Muriel turned to them with a sweet smile. "Look! Increasing voltage won't make the twitches any stronger now. Do you know the reason for the plateau?"

Muriel asked the demonstrators to help the apprehensive students to form groups and set up their experiments. Only the bravest ones were willing to have their *ulnar nerve* stimulated. Muriel walked among them, helping here and there, offering encouraging remarks, discussing and explaining. Patiently, she was guiding them towards understanding how skeletal muscle works, with logical explanations supported by elegant and crisp evidence.

***

Time went by, and summer came again. Muriel was telling me about her rather successful year, at least at work. She published two good papers, her grant application was successful, and she was voted one of the most popular lecturers by the students. She got rather thin, however, owing to the affair with the erratic professor.

"I know I should have known better, but I guess wishful thinking knows no reason", she confessed.

After his return from the conference, he cooled down considerably, and reproached her for letting him down in his hour of need.

"I tried to explain to him how difficult it was for me to leave work at that time. He said he understood, but I could see he was still angry."

Then he came to her with a story about his need for more space. He misses his family, he told her, and still doesn't know if he has done the right thing. "But you are and always will be my best friend," he told her.

"That doesn't sound too promising," I remarked cautiously.

"I know," Muriel said. "We don't see each other much nowadays. He often comes to the lab to seek my advice on various scientific topics, quite ridiculous, don't you think? Is he just checking up on me? He invited me to give a seminar in his department. I agreed but I shouldn't have done. It only makes me sick."

"Yes, you have lost a lot of weight!"

"It's *peristalsis*, smooth muscle contractions. Each time I pass his door, I must rush to the loo. My guts are working away. We can't control our autonomic nervous system, can we? I ought to find another route to my office."

***

"What does it all mean?" Muriel asked me some months later. She had just seen the professor with another woman, a woman from another nearby department. Instead of being upset, she didn't feel anything! Anything at all, except a sense of liberation.

"I was so happy it wasn't me," she said. "I felt so sorry for that woman. What does it all mean? One moment you are so concerned, entangled in someone's life, you are the dearest Muriel. And then it all fizzles out as if it never existed.

All that exhausting turmoil for nothing. Why do I have to have such mayhem in my life when all I want is calm and serenity?"

"Muriel, you are not the only one," I told her. "Look at me! …. Anyhow, you look much better now than when I last saw you."

She smiled and adjusted the straps on her surprisingly sexy blouse.

A relationship with a kite

MISSION IMPOSSIBLE
1994

Drown your sorrows in the blue lagoons of my eyes.
A cultured European lady, slim 5'6",
is looking for a kind-hearted, thoughtful man, 45-55,
who loves to be alive.

27 June 1994

Dear Blue Lagoons,

Some ads should be censured! And yours is nearly one of them! How many a man with a predilection for blue eyes, fail to respond to an ad like yours?

Whether to dissolve my cares or simply drown in those deep lagoons of yours, only time and circumstance may tell! The prospect of either might well overwhelm any man with a hint of romance in his soul! But how could any such not chance his heart and his soul in such a cause? Men have abandoned life for less!

Within your chosen words, delicious though they are, is little said. That you are of continental origin is written. But whence came you, dear lady, and where did you acquire such imagery? Within your lines, do I detect some Celtic magic, perhaps? For Celts may have eyes of clearest blue. But then, the word "Continent" inclines one to think of different origins.....Conjecture adds spice to your mystery.

My eyes are neither blue, nor brown, but a blend of grey and green, tinged with gold. Whether eyes of grey and green and gold sit easily with those of clearest blue I cannot presume. You can consider that better than I. And should you think it strange for my eyes to be as they are, it is no mystery: I was born in the year of the Tiger.

But eyes are nothing without the inner soul they do display and the setting they enjoy. Though my soul remains great and romantically inclined, I judge the setting less than once it was! I am 56, six foot, divorced, and generously built. The hair has silver-turned, and where once was hair, shines forth over-much pate, I do confess. Perhaps such truth may disincline you to allow me to gaze into those eyes of clearest blue, to drown in dark pools, in those deep lagoons?

I await your judgment. In manus tuas, domina! I swim or drown or fade away at your command! The phone is by your hand, Ring me!

Yours John

9 July 1994
Dear John,

Thank you for your quite splendid letter. It stands out above the other replies as the roar of a tiger stands out amongst the twittering of sparrows, or as a noble mountain rises above the surrounding hills and lagoons. I am flattered and touched that my few words could move you to such eloquence but somewhat dismayed, I must confess, at your address. Devon! And I live in London! And though my inner soul soars to the heavens at your words, such a distance separates us! So many miles between my blue and your grey, green, and gold. Maybe it seems strange and inappropriate to make an obstacle of something so trivial. Maybe the prospect of our eyes meeting should pull us together whatever the distance. I can't conceal, however, that there is a practical edge to my Bohemian background (a clue!!). And though my heart pounds and my blue lagoons swell with tears at your words, I cannot envisage a sensible relationship with a man living so far away, even if that man is a poet and a tiger!

However, if in your peaceful home in the depth of Devon you might again feel the fluttering of Muses' wings, please do not hesitate, and let them guide your pen. I shall be delighted to hear the echoes of tranquil Devonian hills in the mad rush of the seething Metropolis.

Best wishes Helena

14 July 1994

Dear Helena,

So the eyes that I would like to drown within are Bohemian! Wonderful! A picture comes before my eyes: all mountains, valleys, streams, trees, all claiming their way to reach a sky of crystal blue. But as you say, so far away. Fret not, however, I do know where London is, for I was born near there - some 15 miles away. Someday, some way, we will meet – a delightful prospect.

While I am writing this, I have in the background on the stereo Max Bruch's Violin Concerto that brings deep and wonderful memories: velvet sky and stars like diamonds, a tropical African night. It was my first wife who introduced me to Bruch nearly 30 years ago. She was tall and blonde and English-born, though she was at that time a Hungarian baroness. She ended up in Swaziland on some business, while I was there serving Queen and country as an Education Officer. A beautiful woman, a tropical night, what a heady potion!

But I digress. Back to London. It just needs a bit of organising. For a man who regularly drives thousands of miles a year, London is not impossible. So – my Bohemian, meet we will, and as soon as your wild social programme permits.

With an ad like yours, you will have had many replies from totally wonderful men. But how many of them have soul? I hope there could be a small niche in your life for me. Write or ring, I but wait, disconsolate – but hopeful. Anything is possible.

Yours ever, John

20 July 1994

Dear John,

You must have travelled a lot: Swaziland, Bohemian streams, Kent, Devon, tropical nights, Hungarian baroness – my head is spinning!

This is just a brief note to let you know that I too am getting ready for some travels. In two days' time, I will be off to Uzbekistan, so now am busy packing and organising. I can't wait to get away since I have had a rather tough time at work lately. I wish you were right about my wild social programme! It is wild indeed, except it isn't social, but mostly related to work. So, I am not exactly mingling with countless wonderful, but soul-less, men. How boring, you may think. Not really, I have a kind of love-hate relationship with work.

I shall write more when I get back. Meanwhile, have a good summer.

Best wishes Helena.

26 July 1994

Dear Helena,

Uzbekistan is a little far for a quiet tête-à-tête! Both I and any bent-kneed camel would be exhausted by the time we arrived, and your blue lagoons would be long gone.

But you raise a question in my simple little mind. What pray is Helena doing in Uzbekistan? A holiday? Possibly – but more like something else. Maybe business? At least that would be my instinct. It makes me wonder what Helena is about. Perhaps I will find out one day.

Had we time to meet and talk, there is so much to tell. Some would interest and some would bore you. My poor pen can but outline any thoughts, only my voice, my presence, can add timbre and fabric and substance to the little that my pen can offer.

But two little nuggets: First: a colleague and I are contemplating a joint venture with two Czech gentlemen (a food company). A little coincidence for you to contemplate. Nothing is signed yet, but we expect to complete soon. Secondly, my wife's petition for divorce proceeds – I will have the decree absolute by the end of August. There is a long story behind all this, but I will skip it. Let me just say this: what she began, she will complete. Somehow, somewhere, sometime, some ten years ago, I lost her love. I never did find out why, but it happened. But then, she never did have taste! Or perhaps, I should have said she had lost whatever taste she had had. Tiger yawns.

And so, new beginnings beckon. How wonderful it would be to have a friend called Helena, with those eyes of Bohemian blue. Even if she will keep me at arm's length. Within my heart there flickers a little flame, a tinge of hope that one day....

Yours John

12 August 1994

Dear John,

Sorry to hear you are having hard time right now. However, you sound like you are one of those eternal optimists who know that life just goes on. As for your Czech venture, I wish you good luck!

Uzbekistan was a holiday. I have not met a single camel there, but many mules and sheep and handsome shepherds. They all spoke Russian, which I speak reasonably well, so I could chat with them all. It was fun to be in such an exotic country and to be able to communicate with everyone. I have spent one week walking in the mountains, nearly 4000m high, and one week admiring Samarkand and Bokhara. After this, the pulsating city life seems rather futile.

Your instinct was wrong, I am afraid. I am not a businessperson at all. I am an academic, who spends her life inside, what some may call, an Ivory Tower, though I would disagree with that. More like inside a running wheel, it seems to me. But any more details would, I fear, bore the Devonian Tiger. Just to say, there are days when I spend 14 hours inside that wheel. So, I need these little escapes badly! I will be getting off the treadmill again for a few days to do a bit of cycling in Essex with my friends. And there will also be a few days in Berlin in September.

Let the river Axe carry all your problems away and dump them into Seaton Bay.

Best wishes Helena

31 October 1994

Dear Helena,

You must have wondered what on earth happened to me – all this time and nothing heard! To be honest, I have been very depressed for some time, not clinically, but down in the dumps. There have been many reasons for this, but once in such toils on one's own, it is very difficult to get out of them again. I had thought I had made it in the spring, but then the dumps came back again in the summer and, to some extent, are with me still.

I won't bore you with all the sorry details. Suffice it to say that being downcast was due to circumstances, over which I had little control. I know I must get on with my life and turn my back on the past, but it goes against all that I hold dear: commitment and loyalty. It is hard to turn my back on a relationship that meant so much, just because the other one said it was over. All the 'if onlys; and 'what ifs' came to the fore again, but the outcome of all my soul searching will always be the same: all totally negative… "Just forget it!", can be the only true answer. I was a fool, as everyone told me at the time, some ten years ago. And I feel like an even greater idiot now. How could I delude myself for so long?

Business-wise, things have not been great either. The rest has been a mess of minor niggles, which I could cope with if all else was on song. As it is, they became an aggravation out of all proportion.

So, my girl, instead of a White Knight in burnished armour bright, astride his charger, its nostrils flaring and tail switching, before you lies upon his knees, dusty, his surcoat torn and ragged-edged, a true and trusty fellow, but with armour rusted and no little battered and cut about. His shield dented and his helmet all askew.

Not much of a hero, this fellow. So, Helena, please forgive the break in contact.

Over recent months, you have travelled much, Samarkand and Essex and Berlin. Why? Is there a connection? I am much intrigued. Ring or write to me, that is if my recent attack of glooms has not quite put you off.

I trust you are well and in good spirits,

Best wishes John

14 November 1994

Dear John,

I am sorry you are still having such hard times, plunged into the depths of despair.

Although I am the last person to dispense pearls of wisdom, I think that bad things in life can often lead to unexpected turns for the better. One can learn about oneself, cast a critical eye over one's life, and think about how and what to change. Sometimes, disasters are necessary to kick one to action, out of the staleness. "Just forget it" is not a good idea; better to learn from it before setting out on another journey. A good theory, isn't it? I know that practice is much harder. But life and hopes do go on, things will be all right again.

Best wishes Helena

15 December 1994

Dear Helena,

Just a very brief note to thank you for your recent letter and to wish you a Happy Christmas

Even though I am not looking forward to this Christmas – the first time I have been away from my children – I am actually feeling better than I was some weeks ago. No doubt, brightened up by your letter! Keep them coming!

I hope it may be possible to meet sometime in the New Year. We may be opening an office in the London area soon – so who knows?

I hope you have a jolly time - all those chaps losing their hearts to those blue lagoons. And watch out for the mistletoe!

Best wishes, Happy Christmas, John

20 December 1994

Dear John,

Merry Christmas to you too.

As for me, I am off to Sicily for Christmas with my son, my friend, and her son.

You must be wondering: What is the connection? Are the blue lagoons involved in spying? Dragging all those men, so eager to drown in them, under skillfully prearranged mistletoes? And then? Who knows what frightful predicaments might ensue? I envisage those incredulous tiger's eyes, grey, green, and golden, wide open in bewilderment. And then, half-closed in mistrust.

Well, no, I have other plans and another idea for jolly times. Dear John, my intuition tells me that we are not destined for each other. I enjoyed your letters and appreciated your very impressive gift of gab. I do genuinely emphasise with you; I have been through a similar turmoil (as have many others). I am glad if I succeeded, at least a little bit, in brightening your subdued spirits. Perhaps you will surprise yourself and enjoy the coming festive season much more than your gloomy expectations imply. I hope you will find peace of mind and happiness before too long.

Best wishes for a Happy New Year, Helena

A Woman on the Treadmill and a sad Tiger

FIFTY
1995

You wake up on Friday at 6 am. "Happy birthday to me!" you sing quietly to yourself. You feel like a historical monument. Fifty! It can't be true, such numbers refer to elephants, whales, or turtles.

As usual, you worry about work. About grants. You haven't got one and you feel it's not fair. You have done well and published good papers, but still nothing. Your grant application has been rejected. You can't face writing any more applications and wasting your precious time. Instead, you could be doing all those exciting experiments that you had planned. Of course, you know that everyone could say that, but that's no comfort. You don't want to be a fundraiser instead of a scientist. You are too tired and too disappointed to talk yourself into bouncing right back - as is expected of you. "Why do you make such a fuss about it?" your friends ask. "You have got a job, haven't you? You are OK!"

But what about recognition and work satisfaction?

You worry about your sons. You can hear your pious ex's familiar phrases coming out of their mouths.

"You are losing so much because of your materialistic thinking," your sons tell you. "You have been brainwashed into atheism! You are too limited, too prosaic!"

They feel sorry for you. And what's more! They may even be anxious about you ending up in hell. The distance between you and them seems to be getting unsurmountable.

You also worry about the men that you are meeting. Your hopes won't be crushed just yet, so you are still looking for that implausible perfect partner. Part of you enjoys it, your adrenalin rises, and the air is full of possibilities. You listen carefully, ask polite questions, and wish they too would ask questions and listen to you. You learn a lot about yourself and about others. But not much luck there either. And it's so exhausting! You are tired, it almost feels like having another job, another chore.

You have started seeing Mrs K to sort yourself out. You talk, she listens, and sometimes she comments. It is a luxury worth paying for. "Allow yourself some fun, don't take things so seriously," she says. "Don't look for perfection, just for good enough. Don't argue with your children, you can't discuss faith. Just be there for them."

Well, here you are, fifty today! You are taking a day off to prepare for tomorrow's party. An intermezzo, an escape, a V sign, proof that you are still alive and kicking, that you can still rise and shine. You have invited some fifty people. Each of them will bring food, but today, you are going to cook anyhow. Your potato salad is always a hit. And so is your unbeatable trifle. There will be your sons and your niece and cousins, your work friends, cycling and walking friends, your students, neighbours, Czech friends, and Chitra with her daughters and her 93-year-old mother Avni. Chitra's ex-husband Sumeet, the grumpy painter, won't be coming, thank goodness - that could be awkward. You wonder how all these people will mix. You are chopping vegetables, music on full blast.

The party is over. You wake up late Sunday morning reviewing the event. You feel it was worth the effort. People enjoyed themselves. The buzz is still with you. You were running around with coats, flowers, food, and presents, enthusiastically dancing in between. One of the students played piano, Chitra's daughters sang beautifully. Towards the end, the Czechs took over and the singing degenerated into a jolly smuttiness. The 93-year-old granny Avni sat on the sofa in the corner and observed it all with great gusto. As she was leaving, she said "Coming here was wonderful for me. I have so much enjoyed watching you all dance!" She was almost in tears. You thought it was perhaps the best, the most moving thing about the party.

You give yourself another birthday treat. A short trip to Austria to do some cross-country skiing in snowy woods. You shoot out like a bullet along a Langlauf track, releasing all that energy that had been chained to your computer for months. Feeling blissfully happy with snow, pine trees, space, and movement. And then back to work.

Some encouragement comes when you get an invitation to a meeting in Hamburg from the German Cell Biology Society. Why wasn't there an invitation from a British one? You wonder if you have made enemies. You are telling yourself off for paranoia and despondency. It's a love-hate relationship with your work. When you try to live a little, as well as work, you feel guilty and exhausted. But when you just work and work, you feel depressed. You write more grant applications. After six months, another one gets rejected, but this time it just washes over you. You don't want to be in a race. You will have to write another one, but no rush, one thing after another. Three more applications get rejected before finally, after 18 months of applying, you get a grant. By then, the momentum is lost, and you accept the slower pace. Let go of your high ambitions, scale down your dreams. Just do your best.

**

I have almost forgotten how frantic life was at fifty. One usually remembers the good times rather than those full of agony and despair. A quarter-century later, I can't help feeling sympathy for the fifty-year-old me. And I know that I was not the only one. I commiserate with all those fifty-year-old mums, then and now, trying to cope with work, men, hot flushes, and difficult adolescents. Take it easy, girls! It doesn't have to be perfect. Just good enough. Be kind to yourselves.

KEEP CALM YOU'RE ONLY 50

A HEAVY SHOWER
2009

Nine o'clock at night and pouring rain. 'Where is she?' This afternoon, my friend Angela cycled off to visit her family. It was her grandson's fifth birthday.

Little Johnnie was into cars and Lego. Angela splashed out on a large set with a garage, a breakdown truck and an assortment of cars, tools, and repairmen. She wrapped the Lego box with great care, adding amusing personalized stickers. Great Work! Speedy Worker. Well Done, Johnnie! She inserted loving messages into the box. Happy Birthday, darling Johnnie!

Angela's daughter Jane lived with her family in a Sussex village. We decided to rent a cottage near them for a few days around Johnnie's birthday. Angela thought this was the best plan: we would do a bit of cycling and some walking, meet our friends from Lewes, and she would be able to visit the family without imposing on them. She always worried about being a nuisance.

Jane's house was some seven miles away from our cottage, not a great distance. Angela said she would cycle on the quiet country lane to avoid the shorter, but very busy main road. The lane was hilly but much safer. She did take her waterproofs but was not prepared for this kind of downpour. She didn't like any fuss and used to laugh at my pannier bags full of the 'just in case' stuff. She liked to travel light.

It was getting dark. 'Where is she?' I fretted. She may have decided to stay overnight with the family. But then surely, she would have let me know. I didn't get any reply from her mobile and had no contact for her daughter. I had already considered phoning the police when finally, Angela appeared on the doorstep. She was drenched, her face ashen. She stood there speechless like a distressed, injured animal.

"Oh my God, Angela, what happened?"

She was shaking and remained silent. I helped her out of her wet clothes, brought a woolly blanket and made some tea.

"I can't believe I am still alive!" she said finally. "There was hysterical laughter, soon followed by a burst of tears. "Oh my God, oh my God!"

"Did something happen to you on the bike? Or at the party?"

Angela was sobbing. "It was terrible! The whole afternoon was just terrible." She was getting through a box of paper hankies. "Why? What have I done to them?"

I met Angela's family only once, last year, at her garden party. Jane had two small children and worked as a part-time teacher; her hands were full. Peter, the son-in-law, was a dentist, a confident young man with strong opinions and few doubts. Quite a contrast to Angela, who had to question and examine whatever she did. Perhaps also what others did. She may have said too much at some point. I noticed a certain unease between her and the son-in-law but I didn't pay much attention to it then. The party was a success, Peter was full of charm, chatted to me amicably and I had a good time. Now, looking at that heap of unhappiness in front of me, I realized how unaware I was.

"What happened, Angela? Do you want to tell me?"

"Can you bear to listen to it?" Angela drank a second cup of tea, slowly calming down. "It's just another mother-in-law story. There are so many of them around. I don't want to bore you."

"Go on, I am listening."

"You know how cautious I am when I have any dealings with Jane's family. I feel Peter is just sitting there, waiting to jump at me as soon as I do anything wrong. He doesn't say much, it's his body language. Rolling his eyes, leaving the table abruptly, avoiding any eye contact, avoiding any conversation with me. I might as well be invisible. When Johnnie opened my present, Peter took the box away and said, 'Let's not make a mess right now, shall we?' Johnnie wasn't even allowed to look inside. Jane said nothing, she didn't want to upset Peter. She never challenges him. I could hardly find any time to talk to her in private. Anyhow, she always seems to avoid it. She knows it upsets Peter because he just assumes we talk about him."

"She must have been very busy though, with all those kids and mums around," I tried to put a word in, but Angela was in full flow now. Colour returned to her face as she got more agitated and angrier.

"It's always like this. When I am around, sooner or later there will be a scene. Peter just wants full control of her. Anyway, I just sat there quietly eating my piece of that bloody cake. Then I forced myself to make small talk with Peter's mother and tried to be helpful when the children played 'Pass the Parcel'. I asked for a cup of coffee and Jane just pointed me to the kettle. Yes, I know

Jane was busy. But then, why was Peter happily pouring tea for other mums and grannies? I felt totally unwelcome. And it was beginning to rain. And soon it was bucketing. 'Well, I better be going before it gets dark', I said."

"You could have asked for a lift. It would have taken them just a few minutes."

"Never! I was in no state to do that. I was hurting all over. And to add insult to injury, they didn't offer. They could see the downpour; they knew I came on my bike. 'I better be going', I said. And nothing. 'Good to see you, Mum,' Jane said and nudged Johnnie to say thank you for the present. The one he wasn't allowed to look at. There was a hardly perceptible nod from Peter."

"That was mean! I am so sorry. But still, Angela, I think you should have – in front of everyone - asked for a lift. You could have said 'I can't cycle back in this weather. Can I get a lift please?' They couldn't have refused you."

"Perhaps I should have asked but at the time, I couldn't. I didn't mean to play a martyr. I think I was just so shaken I couldn't act rationally." Angela covered her face and there was a long silence. We sat quietly together.

"I couldn't face all those hills, so I decided to use the main road," she continued. "That road is a nightmare at any time, but Friday evenings are the worst. I can't believe I am still alive!"

"I was so worried about you; I nearly called the police."

"There was a stream of heavy traffic, massive lorries with their huge tyres whooshing and splashing, I was soon covered in mud. The oncoming traffic was blinding me. I had my lights on, but I couldn't see much anyhow. My waterproofs were getting caught in the gears. I felt as if that ferocious, dirty stream of traffic was going to devour me. Like those machines that gobbled up Charlie Chaplin in 'The Modern Times' film. I stared at the road edge right in front of me, 'Just keep going. Just keep going! It will soon be over,' I talked to myself. A self-preservation instinct? Or a death wish? I don't know. Let's go to bed. Thank God I have taken my sleeping pills with me."

The next morning was bright and sunny. The damp hills, bathed in the rising mist, were the only reminder of yesterday's heavy downpour. We left our bikes behind and walked over the dreamy rolling South Downs.

"Let's have a good time today!" Angela said.

We didn't speak about yesterday. We had lunch at an old pub in Alfriston and then did some more walking, busying ourselves with maps and routes. The frenzied, thundering lorries were miles away. We bought some wine, pizza, and salad for the evening.

Just as we opened the bottle and settled down, Angela's mobile rang. "Hello Jane," she answered and walked away to the kitchen area.

"Yes, I am fine, thanks. No, no, you are not disturbing anything. How did the rest of the party go? Did you stay up much longer?"

"Yes, it was a lovely party. I am glad Johnnie liked his presents."

"Well, I got a bit wet yesterday, but I'm OK now. It was so nice to see you all. You must all come for dinner soon."

"You too take care, bye-bye."

Angela came back to the table and had a sip of her glass. "Don't look at me like that," she said as she tucked into her cold pizza.

"Well, you could have…."

"I know. Don't say another word. Please. To our health!"

We raised our glasses and settled down in front of the telly to watch the next gripping episode of 'Wallander'.

Can't believe I am still alive!

UNCLE BOB'S VISIT

2014   (as remembered by my nephew Pepi)

Just as I expected. As soon as we had settled down at a restaurant in Soho, Uncle Bob started to harass the young blonde waiting at our table.

"You are very pretty, you know that don't you?"

I noticed Mum and Auntie Helena exchanging glances. Bob is their first cousin, but for me he's always been Uncle Bob, notorious for his penchant for young girls. He lives in New York, working in the 'rag trade' as he calls it. We have heard shocking stories of his escapades with numerous young ladies. Each time, Uncle Bob is convinced he has found the love of his life. He will show us photos of himself laughing happily in the embrace of one or another, declaring dreamily "She is so beautiful, I adore her."

Uncle Bob is mid-sixties. He looks after himself, goes to a gym, eats salads and wears black polo-neck tops. Whatever hair is left on his skull is cleanly shaved just like that of Uncle David, my real uncle, now known as Venerable Dharmakara. In fact, the resemblance between these two cousins is quite remarkable considering that one is a Buddhist monk and the other a rag trade mafioso.

Auntie Helena forcefully pushed the menu in front of Bob's nose to stop him from harassing the poor girl.

"Let's have a look at the menu, shall we?"

He beamed a huge smile at her. "Mishpocheh!" he exclaimed. "I love you all."

Auntie smiled back at him. "Isn't it lucky that the visit of my sister and Pepi from Prague just happened to coincide with your business trip? And so here we are, all together in London."

Uncle Bob's smile continued to beam. "You are my guests, choose whatever you like."

"No! It's our treat," Mum protested. "We have invited you, Bob."

"Don't argue with him, Mum," I whispered. "No fuss."

"Pepi," Uncle Bob turned to me. "You must be starving. Shall we go for the Deluxe Set Menu for the four of us? That'll be nice and simple."

"Nice and simple? Don't be crazy, Bob." Auntie Helena opposed. "It's got seven courses. We won't be able to eat all that."

The pretty waitress re-appeared. "Shall I give you some more time?"

Uncle Bob aimed his grin at her. "Where are you from, sweetie?"

"Ukraine" she replied curtly.

"Whereabouts in Ukraine?" Bob persevered.

"Polyanka, you wouldn't have heard of it. It's a small village near Lviv."

"I do know Lviv. Actually, some of my family comes from that region."

"Really? What a surprise!" She gave him a sweet smile. "Small world!"

Poor thing, I thought, what else can she do? She's got to be polite. Still, I wished I was better at chatting up girls.

"What's your name?" Bob carried on.

"Nastya."

"Nastya, Nastyenka, how nice."

"Have you decided?" Nastya asked.

"I'll just have a couple of Dim Sums, that'll be plenty for me." Mum said.

"Nonsense, this is a family feast." Uncle Bob beckoned to the Ukrainian girl. "Nastyenka, we have decided. Nice and simple for us, nice and simple for you: four Deluxe Set Menus. And, darling, can we have some crispy seaweed while we wait?"

Another girl appeared to inquire about our drinks. She was gorgeous, a Hispanic type, long dark hair, deep brown gazelle eyes, slim and elegant. Again, Uncle Bob was in his element.

"We are all having Deluxe Set Menus", he broadcasted, "What kind of deluxe wine would go with it? What do you think, love?" he drooled over her.

She was young, but not too young, late thirties. That would be a nice age for me, since I am getting on too. I am pushing fifty, a chilling thought.

I noticed a pendant she was wearing; it was the logo of the Football Club Barcelona. Not that I am a football fan. I recognized it only because very recently I had watched a TV programme about FCB.

"Are you from Barcelona?" I took a chance. "Into football? Thumbs up for FCB! Barcelona Soccer is great." I carried on although Uncle Bob had already started to inquire about her name.

"Yes, it is." She agreed, happily smiling at me. "Yes, I am from Barcelona."

Then she answered Uncle Bob. "My name is Valeria. Here is the wine list, perhaps some dry white wine?"

Mum and Auntie Helena managed to dissuade Bob from ordering the most expensive bottle. We all settled for Tiger beer, fine with me.

When Valeria came back with our drinks, she tapped my shoulder. "Did you know that FCB also has a women's team?" she asked me.

"Of course," I lied. "I am a great fan of theirs."

"Well done, Pepi!" Uncle Bob commented. "You are a fast learner."

Sipping our beers and munching the seaweed, we began to discuss the family.

"How is your little daughter, Bob?" asked Mum.

That was clumsy of her, I thought, considering that Bob's fatherhood was never fully established. Despite this, Bob's Mum, my Great Aunt Jusia, adores the girl and showers her with presents. But the girl's mother allows only minimal contact between the little girl and her maybe Grandmother. It'd be so easy to resolve the whole issue if only Bob had agreed to a DNA paternity test. But he is in no great hurry. He knows that Jusia would find it hard to cope with a negative outcome. Her little granddaughter is the apple of her eye.

"Thank you for asking, Sandra, the little one is fine. Not so little anymore, she'll be ten next month."

Bob decided to change the subject and turned to my Auntie. "Helena, you became a Granny recently, didn't you? How does that feel?"

"It's wonderful!" Helena said with a big smile. "Not so recently though! I have got three grandchildren now!" She started to rummage in her bag to get some photos of her grandchildren.

I knew exactly what would follow. While Auntie Helena was passing the pictures around, Mum directed her reproachful gaze at me.

"My sister is lucky," Mum said. "No such luck for me. My children are nowhere near to producing any offspring." She gave a deep sigh. "I have almost given up all hope."

"Come on, Sandra!" Uncle Bob grinned mischievously. "Give him a chance! He isn't even fifty yet, still young!"

"Thank you, Uncle, for saying that" I said.

"I know what it feels like." Uncle Bob commiserated. "Unwanted advice, meddlesome questions…"

"Constant disapprovals, heavy-handed suggestions," I complemented.

"No offense my dear cousin," Uncle Bob wrapped his arm around Mum's shoulder and laughed disarmingly. "We understand each other, don't we, Pepi?" We all laughed, and all the more so because both Nastya and Valeria were approaching with a trolley full of our deluxe goodies.

The starters would have been more than enough, but they were followed by Peking Duck pancakes and then beef and chicken and prawns and vegetables, all very delicious. Bob ate very little and asked for an extra salad to avoid unwelcome fats and carbohydrates. As usual, Mum picked warily at this and that, leaving most of the food on her plate. Thus, it was left mainly to me and Auntie Helena to prevent waste. We tried our best but still, we couldn't manage it.

"I can't bear to waste all that wonderful food," auntie Helena was almost in tears, "but I am bursting!"

"Wasting it would be a sin," Mum agreed.

"What shall we do?" They both panicked.

"My dear cousins, don't you worry," Uncle Bob reassured them. "We shall ask for a doggy bag."

"What's that?" I wondered. Uncle Bob duly explained.

"That's embarrassing!" I protested. "You can't do that in a posh place like this."

"Not at all," Uncle Bob said. "Of course you can. It'll make a lovely lunch for you tomorrow. Nastyenka will be happy to sort it out for you, won't you, my dear?" He beckoned to her.

"Would you like to see the dessert menu?" she asked. We just burst out laughing.

"No, thanks. Nastyenka, that will be it. Can you pack the rest of the food for the ladies?" He asked for the bill and inquired about the best way to leave the tip. On the card? In cash?

Both Mum and Auntie Helena made a feeble attempt to contribute, but Uncle Bob had already got up and walked to the bar with his credit card. There he engaged in a long conversation with Nastya and Valeria, occasionally glancing in my direction. They were chatting, laughing, gesticulating. What could he possibly be telling them?

How does he do it? I wish I had the skill. Complimenting their looks? Nastya's silky blonde hair, Valeria's smooth flowing dark mane. Throwing glances of admiration over their figures? Nastya's is rounded and full, Valeria's slender and willowy. Gazing into their eyes? Promising treats? I am in no position to do that. One look at scruffy me and they will think again. While Uncle Bob oozes confidence and affluence, I dribble diffidence and poverty. But would I like to change places with Uncle Bob? No way. I like my freedom, my lone wolf existence up in the Jizera mountains. I don't mind that my cottage is a mess, at least Mum thinks so. I wish she would stop interfering. OK, it's basic, it doesn't offer any luxuries, but I do what I like there, paint, write, walk in the woods and I am happy. I know every forest footpath, every rock and stream, I am a part of that landscape. There are some female visitors occasionally, of course. But I don't rave about every single one of them the way Uncle Bob does. Anyhow, my visitors don't want to live like me. Sooner or later, they start talking babies, homes, security .... Well, sometimes I think I could do with some of it, but I'm not sure. I don't think I'm made for that sort of stuff.

I became certain that Uncle Bob and the girls were talking about me. Valeria even smiled and waved her hand in my direction. Soon Uncle Bob came back with two carrier bags full of little plastic boxes containing the remnants of our Deluxe. His eyes twinkled with happiness as if he had just won Olympic Gold. He put his arms around the shoulders of both Mum and Auntie Helena.

"My dear ladies! The night is young and Nastyenka and Valeria will soon be free. They have kindly accepted my invitation to join me at Ronnie Scott's, my favourite Jazz Club. How about you, Pepi? Will you too be my guest? My dear ladies, will you excuse young Pepi here for the rest of the evening?"

"That's amazing!" I couldn't believe my luck. "Thanks, I love the idea."

"But Bob," Mum protested. "It's nearly eleven!"

"So?" Uncle Bob raised his eyebrows.

"But..."

"Don't you worry, my lovely cousins. Pepi will be safe and sound. He'll be back home in the early hours so that you can share the Chinese lunch." He placed the carrier bags, one each, into Mum's and Auntie's hands.

"It's OK, Sandra, it's OK," Auntie Helena continued to reassure her sister in Czech. "Let him be, he is nearly fifty!"

My hat's off to Uncle Bob. With girls around him, he's got the energy of a frisky billy goat. We had an absolutely great time, all thanks to his oomph and generosity. The girls were friendly and had a good sense of humour. Soon the air began to sparkle. In the small hours, Nastyenka and Bob vanished. It was now up to me and Valeria to finish the bottle of wine and to talk about our lives, about everything under the sun. Under the moon - I should have said, there was a full moon that night. Among other things, I confessed I had never heard of the Barcelona Soccer women's team before. Valeria laughed and said she could tell straight away. As I walked her slowly home through the night streets of London, all kinds of fantasies danced in my head. I felt curiously both relaxed and elated.

Uncle Bob with the girls

"Are you all right?" Mum texted me at nine o'clock in the morning. I was glad she restrained herself and waited until then.

"Yes, I am fine, will be back by noon."

Valeria started her shifts at eleven, so we had time enough for a leisurely breakfast.

We said our goodbyes in front of the Chinese restaurant in Soho. "Oh yes," I said when she asked if I would like to visit her in Barcelona after she returned there. She expects to stay in London for another four months or so, she needs to save enough money to help her pay for her Psychology Course. And "Oh yes," she said, she would love to see my paintings. She has never been to Prague before, but she has heard it's very beautiful. And a trip to the mountains? Well, that would be fun. She doesn't mind roughing it and she loves walking.

"Did you have a nice time?" Mum asked.
"Come on, tell us all," demanded Auntie Helena tactlessly.
"Let me recover first," I said. "I'm quite hungry. "Are we having Chinese for lunch?"
There was plenty in the doggy bags for the three of us to have a splendid meal. I divulged the minimum necessary to satisfy Mum's and Auntie's curiosity.

The phone rang as we were relaxing with our coffee afterwards. It was Uncle Bob inquiring about how I got on.
"Well, I hope to visit Barcelona before the end of the year. And Valeria would love to see Prague. I told her May is the best month to come, the most romantic. How about you?"
"Fantastic!" Bob exclaimed. "Nastyenka managed to get a cover for herself at the restaurant and we are now at

Madame Tussauds. I have just sent you a photo, have a look at your WhatsApp. It's her with Prince William. She thinks I look a bit like him. She is amazing. I have never been in love so much, I'm lost!"

HOLIDAY FELLOWS
2015

"Welcome to Sunny Lodge! Have you travelled from afar? Did you drive?"

"Thank you. From London. No, I came on a train and then a bus."

"Can I help you to your room? Can you manage the steps?"

"Thank you, I'm all right."

"Lucky with the weather, aren't we? Don't forget to fill in the form."

Finally alone, I looked around my room. The window looked out onto a large garden with cedars and daffodils. Flowery curtains fluttering in the breeze, sun-lit hills in the background. A comfortable clean bed with a good reading light above, hot shower, an electric kettle, and a basket full of tea bags, milk sachets, and biscuits. Plenty of drawers, and a large wardrobe. I slowly unpacked my gear, boots, gaiters, anorak, and my waterproof trousers. For the evenings there were a few nice tops to match my black trousers and a pair of light shoes. By four o'clock I had unpacked and was ready for our welcome tea downstairs.

I descended the wide staircase into the common room. People in red velvet armchairs were eating large scones smothered with jam and cream and sipping their tea. There were four couples, three men engaged in a lively conversation, one man sitting quietly on his own, and five single women who raised their expectant eyes as I entered but then again resumed their chatting.

I settled down on a separate chair, savouring the hot scone and observing the guests. Most of them seemed to be in their sixties, one of the four couples much further advanced and one a bit younger, mid-fifties or so. The three men, evidently good friends, were noisily relishing each other's company. One of the five ladies was a blonde in a striking lime-green jacket over immaculate white trousers; she listened to the others with the utmost attention and heartily encouraged the conversation with smiles and approving nods. The lone man appeared quite at ease with his scone and tea, looking around the place with an amused expression. He kept looking at his watch; at five o'clock he jumped up and walked towards our two walking guides.

"Isn't it time for our briefing?"

Here we were: on our best behaviour, determined to have a good time, listening to tomorrow's plans. Our guides were here to make sure that we had fun. They were fit, experienced, responsible, and ready to provide us with safe adventures. They explained tomorrow's routes: the easier and the harder options. I always choose the hard one. That's what I like best, a day of hefty exertion in the hills finished off by a nice hot shower and good food. Bonding with nature and a bit of interesting conversation at dinner time.

At dinner, I sat next to the lone man. His name was Philip.
"So – which walk will you do tomorrow?" I asked him.
"The long one, like you." He turned around to catch the waiter. "Hi, Steve, can you bring me my usual?"
"Do you know him? Have you been here before?"

"Oh yes, I'm an old hand at this place." Philip smiled to himself as if he knew all the local secrets.

"I don't know much of the Peak District. I'm looking forward to it."

"Have you got good solid boots? It will be muddy up there."

"Yes, my boots are well-tested," I assured him.

"And good socks? They are just as important as boots."

"Where do you live?" I asked tentatively.

"Oh, renting at the moment, trying to make my mind up about where to settle down."

"Have you narrowed down your choices yet?"

"No, not yet. We'll see."

I gave up. Obviously, he was a man of few words who liked to keep himself to himself, very impersonal. He was a somewhat stocky man, probably in his late sixties, in good shape, strong and muscular, round-faced with ruddy cheeks and a grey crop of short hair. His eyes would catch a brief glimpse of a person and then quickly dart sideways. A mixture of pomposity and insecurity. He was hard work; so very interested to find out if I use walking sticks. But at least the food was delicious, and we could exchange some remarks about that.

The next day began with a crisp, sunny morning and an invigorating climb. Our walk, the hard one, was to be 12 miles long. Eight of us chose to do it: the three jolly men, Tim and Tanya, one of the four couples - the younger one, the smiling blond lady, Philip and me. The delicate green colours of early spring livened the hills and the dales. We were soon rewarded with wonderful views over the Peak District. Meadows covered with yellow buttercups, white blossoming hawthorns, and lambs. Philip relaxed and talked more easily, pointing out plants, birds or features of the country. We could hear other members of the group exchanging all sorts of personal details, husbands, wives, children, grandchildren, jobs, hobbies, and even information about various items of their thermal underwear.

"Who needs to know all these particulars," Philip grumbled. I wasn't sure whether he meant it as a joke or if he was truly annoyed. We kept to the safe subjects, weather, flora and fauna, and a bit of local history. He was knowledgeable on all these matters.

Philip was well ahead of me now and the blonde lady appeared at my side. Today she wore a luminous pink anorak, black leggings, and a matching polka dot sun hat. Her fingernails were bright pink too. She walked fast, with ease and confidence. A radiant smile never left her face surrounded by peroxide blonde curls.

"What a lovely day!" she said ecstatically. "Isn't it just glorious? Look how well Mam Tor stands out."

"Yes, wonderful," I said. "A great day to be out."

"My name is Angela," she said. "Have you been here before?"

"Nice to meet you, Angela. No, I haven't walked in the Peaks yet. But you seem to know the area well."

"I love these hills. I live in Manchester, so I could have easily come here just for a day. But now that I'm retired, I like to spoil myself a bit."

"That's exactly what I am doing," I said. I could hardly keep pace with this energetic woman. "Have you explored many different places?"

"Oh no, that's not my way. I don't like travelling distances." Angela explained. "All I need is at my doorstep. I just like to treat myself occasionally to a bit of luxury. My life is at home. I keep myself very busy there."

"What do you do?"

"I run three miles every day first thing in the morning. I also do some charity work for RSPCA and teach meditation to dogs and their owners."

"Really? Meditation for dogs? Do they respond?"

"Absolutely! It's wonderful to meditate with animals. Dogs have this healing energy. You can just feel the deep connection they make with their owners during the class." Her smile broadened as she turned to me. "Do you have a dog? Do you practice meditation?"

"No, sorry, I don't have a dog. I have a cat though. And sometimes he likes to be around when I meditate. And I do yoga."

Angela handed me her business card. "Here you are, just in case you decide to get a dog. No cats please, that wouldn't work. But of course, people without dogs can come too. It's so good for you."

I noticed Philip talking to our guide and pointing to his watch again. "Isn't it time for our elevenses?" He must be a very regular sort of chap. As if he wanted to make sure we followed a set of rules of which he was better aware than anyone else. He seemed to keep an eye on our guides to make sure they complied. Our guide Carol was a fifty-something woman, perhaps sixty, no-nonsense, brisk, but easy-going. Her curly hair was coloured purple and she wore shorts despite the biting chill.

"Now then", she said. "We'll stop by the next stile, it isn't far. You'll get a good view from there. Just a ten-minute coffee break. All right?" We all loved her broad local accent.

Angela pulled out a thermos and a small sit mat from her rucksack.

"What a gorgeous view!" She descended gracefully onto her pink mat. "Isn't it just glorious!"

The three men, the jolly friends, made an announcement. One of them, Andrew, was seventy today. They would like to invite the group to join them in celebration on the top of Mam Tor. They pulled out three bottles of champagne from their backpacks, one each, and waved them around. Their chuckling suggested they had started merrymaking already.

"Happy birthday Andrew," everyone shouted. "What better way to celebrate?"

"We are going to let our hair down!" they kept saying shaking their heads, although all three of them were quite bald.

Two hours later, the group reached the top of Mam Tor and unpacked their lunch boxes. Andrew put a funny hat on, and his two friends ran around pouring bubbly into plastic beakers. Especially for the occasion, Andrew brought a crystal glass goblet for himself and was clinking it with everyone's plastic.

"Don't be shy," he said to Angela. "Have some more, it's my birthday. I need a kiss." He embraced her and then proceeded towards the others.

"Happy birthday to me," Andrew shouted. "I need a kiss." He was embracing all of us and shouted, half crying, half laughing. "How did it happen? Where have all the years gone?"

All of us kissed him back and hugged him with great enthusiasm and empathy. Even Philip smiled and hugged. Andrew was from Southampton, a retired lecturer in Philosophy; one of his friends was an IT manager from Aberystwyth, the other a building engineer from Lincoln. The three men had met on a previous holiday some years ago and had continued meeting each other yearly at various locations ever since.

Mam Tor and Peveril Castle

    We continued via the Great Ridge towards Peveril Castle. There Philip came into his own, telling us endless stories about William Peveril, who was the favourite of William the Conqueror. Tim and Tanya didn't listen to him and chatted together.
    "I guess they have something more important to attend to," Philip muttered angrily and carried on until the guide Carol interrupted.
    "Enough said, my love. We better get on then. Our bus will be waiting for us at the Hope Station."

"You know a lot about Derbyshire," I tried to cheer Philip up.

"It was rude to natter while I was talking," he said. "What's the point of rushing around with your eyes and ears closed?"

"I am sure no offense was meant."

"Travelling is learning. Anyway, that's how I do it. My bucket list is all about travelling and learning."

"Your bucket list? Aren't you too young for that?"

"One is never too young for that," he said quietly and rushed down the path, immersed in his own world.

Philip's mood lifted when we reached the Hope Station. "Oh, hello Bill!" He greeted the bus driver as an age-old friend. "Long time no see."

"Hi, Philip! Back in the Peaks again?" They shook hands and chatted cheerfully all the way back to Sunny Lodge.

"Have you read anything by Anne Mustoe?" Tanya asked me at dinner time.

"Yes, what an amazing woman!" I was happy we found a common interest. Philip was sitting at a safe distance at another table, so there wouldn't be any discussion of socks and walking sticks tonight. He was in the company of Andrew and his friends, who continued their noisy celebrations. Philip sat there with his usual pint, watching them, and saying very little. Tanya, Tim, and I spent most of the evening talking about Anne Mustoe, that indomitable school headmistress who, aged 54, decided to give up her job and cycle around the world.

"She was incredible, wasn't she?" I said." A real adventurer."

"We read all of Anne's books and were so impressed by her courage and resolve! We are planning to do something similar," Tim added eagerly.

"We are thinking about it, not quite at the planning stage yet. Tim had already been on the road for three years before we met. Now that our children have both left the nest, he's got itchy feet again and wants to cycle around the world. I am still undecided," Tanya explained.

"I know the feeling," I said. "I often wondered if perhaps one day I could do something like that, perhaps after I have retired. For three or four months in the spring or summer, travelling with essentials only. One doesn't need much in a warm climate."

"I'd prefer a longer time," Tim said. "We could let our house for a couple of years. It can be done; others have done it. A real adventure, not this fainthearted stuff. That's what we were arguing about when Philip went on and on about the two Williams. Tanya thinks I am too restless."

"Yes," Tanya sighed. "Sometimes I wonder. Is Tim just running away from himself? We must have upset Philip. But can't he understand we need some time to ourselves too?"

Back in my room, I thought of the endless inquiries I had made, the talks with experienced cyclists I had had, and the maps I had studied. Yes, I too was dreaming about real adventures. I too admired Anne Mustoe's books. But then I came across a passage, which made me change my mind. Somewhere in South America, Anne encountered a pack of wild dogs; it was a very narrow escape. They had chased the poor brave woman as she cycled up a hill. She dodged them only because she just about managed to get to the top and could then race downhill, away from the beasts.

As much as I love the outdoors, my problem with it is that for me, anything that moves is a threat. I can walk for hours, looking at the hills and trees, skies and waters. Clouds passing, colours changing, branches swaying, leaves and grasses rustling. But come along cows, horses, and even sheep and I get worried. Dogs are the worst. I imagine myself being torn to pieces by a growling Rottweiler, Alsatian, or any odd canine. The idea of me cycling, calves exposed and unprotected, vulnerable, followed by a pack of hungry dogs, alone, nobody around to help me.... I am going uphill of course and no sign of the top at all. There is no escape, the fastest of the pack has gripped my leg already, torn flesh, blood oozing onto the tarmac...... in vain am I shielding my face....

There were of course other issues. No accommodation to be found. Illness. Punctures, weirdoes, rainstorms, heat waves, disorientation. Lonely meals with no one to talk to. Though of course one is likely to meet interesting people when travelling alone. Perhaps even a knight in shining armour might appear one day, helping to mend a puncture or assisting with a crossing of a turbulent stream. A challenge would be good for me, it's just the right balance that I need to find. With these thoughts, I tossed and turned until the morning came.

*****

You get to know people well during walking holidays. There is plenty of time to talk. You don't know their family and friends and they don't know yours. They have not heard your stories twenty thousand times. There is no danger of them spreading gossip among your folks. At the end of the holidays, we usually exchange emails. Sometimes we stay in touch, but most of them appear and disappear, come and go, leaving memories pleasant or unpleasant, clear or vague, or none.

Andrew and his friends suggested we join them next year for another holiday. Indeed, an email arrived two months after we had said goodbye with the details of when and where the three of them would be meeting. Why don't we book as well? The more the merrier. But I had a trip to the Outer Hebrides planned already for those dates. Just as well, the inebriated jolliness can be rather depressing at times.

Neither did I manage to get to Angela's meditation classes, with or without a dog. I often remind myself of her amazing energy. Behind her glamorous looks, there was plenty of resilience. She had four children from three marriages. One husband was abusive, the other an alcoholic and the last one went off with his much younger secretary. But Angela didn't look back. The show must go on. Her example was inspiring.

By pure coincidence, some six or seven years later, I met our guide, Carol, again. She was leading the West Highland Way, a long-distance walk from Glasgow to Fort William, in which I took part. From her, I learned Philip's peculiar story. He was well known among the walk leaders because he simply lived from one organized vacation to another. He always used the same holiday company; the institution became his family. Nobody knew anything about his background. There were rumours that he used to live in

Australia for many years. Sadly, two years ago Philip was found dead in his bed at a hotel in Yorkshire. The managers could not trace any relatives and Philip was buried at the council's expense in Skipton.

Tim and Tanya sent me a postcard from South Vietnam. They were having a great time after six months of cycling through Burma, Thailand, and Laos. I could reciprocate only with a timid postcard from my cycling trip to Tuscany. Another group holiday I am afraid, but wonderful, nevertheless. In the end, I had to be honest and admit to myself that having adventures while being looked after, fed, guided, and entertained, was not such a bad idea after all. And that I was incredibly lucky to be able to do so. I stayed in my comfort zone; challenged, but not exceedingly so.

SOMETHING UPLIFTING
2016

The Slovak presidency of the European Union had just started, and Bratislava was at its best. The capital was cleaned and decked out. There were numerous festivals to liven up the occasion. A festival of organ music was one of the offers. After a long and busy day of sightseeing, I needed something calm, profound, and uplifting so I bought myself a ticket. The organ concert was in St Martin's Cathedral, an ancient building that stands in the Old Town by the Danube River underneath the Bratislava Castle. In the 1970s, a huge 'New Bridge' was built next to it. A motorway, extending from that bridge, passes right in front of the cathedral's spire. To provide space for the motorway a large section of the Old Town, including most of the Jewish quarter, was demolished. However, if you approach the cathedral from the east, you can pretend the highway isn't there.

I entered full of anticipation. A famous Austrian organist was going to play Bach and Mozart and a few jazzy pieces too. There was a beautiful statue of St Martin in the corner: the gallant saint on a mighty horse cutting his own coat to share it with a beggar. A surge of grand organ music soon filled the cathedral space and I immersed myself in it blissfully. But wait a minute! A disconcerting sound of loud pop music could be heard coming in from the outside. The organist continued playing, but the disturbed audience looked at each other in shock. Some people got up and left and gradually many others followed. It seemed unfair to the organist; the intruding noise wasn't his fault. I exchanged glances with a little old lady who sat near me. She had a remarkably expressive, serious face, shortly cropped gray hair and there was a crutch next to her seat. The lady shook her head disapprovingly, but still tried to concentrate and listened to the organ most intensely. As if to say: 'I'm not going to let the organist down.' I took her example and tried to listen to the organ despite the din. The pulsating pop-rock penetrated the walls of the cathedral. Only a few of us sat there until the bitter end.

"What a shame!" I said to the old lady on our way out. "It must have been so frustrating for the organist!"

"It's a disgrace!" she said angrily. "It's all because we have Europe in here now!"

As we emerged out of the cathedral, she crossed herself. She looked at me. I didn't. I wondered - did that upset her? The pop-rock noise was much stronger now; the other concert was just across the river on the so-called 'UFO Beach' next to the 'New Bridge'. Jovial presenters were egging the crowds on via booming loudspeakers.

"Ladies and gentlemen more from the amazing Para Band! Aren't they great?"

"Para, Para, Para!" shouted the crowd.

"Show them how much you like them!"

"More, more, more!" demanded the audience.

"I'm going to write a letter to the mayor," said the lady, who introduced herself as Edita.

"It was very hard to hear anything," I said, "But did you enjoy what you could hear?"

"He was much better with those jazzy parts," she answered without any hesitation. "His interpretation of Bach was somewhat two-dimensional."

It turned out that Edita was herself an organist.

"A woman organist, that's very rare. I'd love to hear all about it. Why don't we have a drink somewhere? May I invite you?"

We found a bar far enough into the Old Town to prevent the Euro-pop noise from reaching us. I ordered a glass of red wine, Edita had tea with honey. She told me about her studies at the Prague Academy of Music. Organ was her love, but after she had finished studying, it was practically impossible to find any work as an organist and a woman organist at that. Moreover, playing organ was always associated with church music and thus strongly discouraged in socialist Czechoslovakia.

"Many precious church organs were deliberately allowed to deteriorate. But that made me even keener to play!"

Edita sought any opportunity to do so. Whenever possible, she got herself smuggled into forgotten old churches and played there for her own pleasure. But to make her living, she played organ at weddings and wrote reviews for music magazines.

"What happened to you?" I asked and pointed to her crutch.

"Oh, that was an accident, some forty years ago. I must have been 36 or so."

Oh dear! I realized she was only five years older than me.

Edita stirred some of the honey into her tea and slowly picked at the rest, savouring every spoonful.

"I was supposed to play at a wedding, but I was late. I jumped off the bus in a great hurry and ran to the church. A huge car hit me." And with some pride she added: "It was a Chrysler!"

Skull smashed, bones broken. She was unconscious for three weeks.

"Doctors were sure I'd die, but I recovered within two months. It was a miracle!" she said passionately.

It was getting close to midnight, but Edita carried on with ever-increasing zeal.

"I had a guardian angel on my side. He helped me to muddle through the next four months that I had to spend in a sanatorium. He was there with me, I talked to him, I could feel his presence...."

"Let's start on our way home," I suggested. "You said your bus stop is near the Blue Church so we are heading in the same direction."

I wondered when the last time was that she could tell her story to anyone.

"Sorry, I didn't ask anything about your life," Edita said as we started to walk towards the Blue Church. "What was your maiden name?"

I told her. and she started to talk about Franz Kafka.

"Have you read Kafka? I like his stories very much, especially The Metamorphosis."

"Yes, I read lots of Kafka and I like him too."

"Are you Jewish?"

"Yes, genetically and in a cultural sense. But I'm not religious, not practicing."

"I used to be interested in Kabbalah when I was younger," Edita said. She looked at me thoughtfully, as if she hoped that –

with a maiden name like mine - I could perhaps explain Kabbalah to her. Then she continued with her questions.

"What was your job?"

I told her I was a biochemist and Edita became really excited. "My friend, the one with whom I studied Kabbalah, had discovered a Molecule of Life! It has miraculous healing powers."

We were getting close to the Blue Church and Edita talked faster and faster. Her friend called the Molecule of Life 'Methuselah' because it was so old. "Very, very ancient," she said. "He was a clairvoyant and knew exactly the right dose for every disease. What do you think of it?"

"Well, I wish I knew what that Molecule of Life was!" I said.

"If only you two could meet! But unfortunately, my friend passed away two years ago."

"I am sorry to hear that, I would have liked to have met him."

Briefly, the thought of my favourite molecule, actin, crossed my mind. The molecule I had spent years working on. Actin is indeed as old as Methuselah, I thought to myself. Should I mention it to Edita? Tell her about that Molecule of Life? I rejected that idea; it was too late for that. We remained silent for a while.

"My friend was a great help to me," Edita sighed.

"You must miss him," I said. We came to Edita's bus stop. "I'll wait with you for your bus."

But Edita insisted she would walk me all the way back to my guest house, never mind her crutch. "Do you have any children?" she asked.

I told her about my sons, and she started to talk about a young man whom she trained. He was her spiritual child. He studied computers but was such a gifted musician! Now he plays organ. They keep in touch. They are very close. She said this with tears in her eyes.

"How nice for you!" I embraced her with affection, a brave and resilient woman.

We stopped by the beautiful Art Nouveau Blue Church. It stood there in the moonlight like a fairy tale castle, decorated with a mixture of folklore and Jugendstil motifs in shades of blue. I loved the detail of a mosaic with a heavenly blue God's eye, staring out of a white triangle, surrounded by blue feathery ornaments. Next to the church was a large school building in a similar style.

"That's where I went to school," Edita said.

"Now I like it even more, it must have been wonderful to be a student in a building like that."

"It was," Edita smiled. "Enjoy your stay in Bratislava."

We parted in a friendly way, but with some sadness, knowing we would never meet again. She went back, protected by her angels, to her flat in Bratislava, and I had to get ready for my next adventure – a walking trip in the Slovak Ore Mountains.

Bratislava Blue Church, detail

ROSH HASHANAH
2017

I worked it out on Google Maps: it shouldn't take me more than 20 minutes to walk from Hendon Thameslink Station to Leah's house. Leah is my 2nd cousin once removed, born and bred in Britain. She invited me to join her family for the Rosh Hashanah festivities.

West Hendon neighbourhood is mainly Muslim. I noticed a crowd of hijabed girls pouring out of a school. After I had reached Hendon Central, I saw many men in black hats and yarmulkes. Just around the corner from Leah's house, a plump lady in a long dark dress emerged from a house looking distressed.

"Can I ask you for a favour?" she called to me.

"Sure," I said. "What is it?"

"It's our holiday today, you see, and I am not allowed to touch any switches. But I need to switch my cooker off. Could you please do it for me?"

"No problem. Where is it?"

She led the way into the house and further on into her kitchen where two gas rings were burning, fully on.

"One, two!" I switched them off. "Here you are!"

"Thank you so much!" She was incredibly grateful. "You understand we can't do that during our holidays."

"No problem at all," I reassured her. I couldn't help being flattered that she chose me - I must look very trustworthy. Little did she know that strictly speaking, I shouldn't be switching off anything either.

However, in my youth I didn't know anything at all about Jewish rules and traditions, having grown up in socialist Czechoslovakia. I didn't even know there was any Rosh Hashanah, Jewish New Year. My knowledge of Jewish life came mostly from books: Franz Kafka, heart-breaking diaries and poems of Jiří Orten, numerous holocaust stories, Jews hiding, escaping, and being hunted. In my mind, Judaism had always been associated with suffering, alienation, and awkwardness.

It was only after meeting my English cousins that I could put some flesh onto these traditions' bones. The first experience – and what a shock - was the invitation to the wedding of Leah and Howard sometime in the early 70s. Howard comes from Scotland. There was a Scottish Pipe Band, men wore both kilts and yarmulkes, and played wedding marches and klezmer music, all mixed together. People talked about 'lovely properties.' How bourgeois, I thought. At that time, 'socialism with a human face' was still a burning concern for me. Soon my preconceptions fizzled out in face of the simple kindness and friendliness of that family. Invitations to Passover and Yom Kippur meals followed, revealing to me for the first time the normal, comfortable, and joyous side of Judaism.

At Leah's house, festivities were in full swing.
"Helena, how nice to see you! Here comes our Czech cousin!"
Leah and her husband Howard greeted me warmly. For Leah, I am the link to her Czech father: Leah's father, Kurt, was my father's cousin. And for me, Leah is the link to, so to speak, Judaism with a human face. Leah's two daughters, Cheryl and

Eve, were also there together with their children, husbands, and in-laws. They were all dressed rather formally, but soon the ladies discarded their high heels and I felt better in my sensible walking shoes, trousers, and a jumper.

Both Leah's daughters take Jewish holy days very seriously. They became very devout during their university years and so would never switch a gas burner on or off during the holidays. Leah made sure that the festive dinner was cooked well in advance so that her daughters wouldn't have to cope with any such issues. Although neither Leah nor Howard is orthodox, they obey the rules in their presence. After I had told them about the gas cooker, a long discussion followed. Was the lady allowed to ask me for help? Or wasn't she?

Leah's daughters have four children each, which meant that the house was overflowing, everybody talking at the same time. The little ones were screaming and demanding chocolate. As the candles were lit and the singing and praying began, the children calmed down for a moment but soon the screaming resumed. Men continued singing, women talked among themselves, and children squabbled. The noise was terrific, but everybody seemed happy and comfortable, doing something they had always done. I was an outsider, an observer, a privileged witness to these rituals that seemed to me bizarre and yet powerful and sustaining, keeping this motley lot together. A part of me envied them, another part knew that I am not made that way.

There was a time when I experimented with being a "New Born Jew." I learned a lot, but it also became clear that I'm not a pious type. Will these eight little cousins of mine continue in the same vein as their parents? With a definite sense of belonging and entirely comfortable with their identity?

Rosh Hashanah Treats

We washed hands; wine and challah were blessed and served. Apples were dipped in honey so that we all would have a sweet year. Then the dinner for twenty people continued as customarily as could be expected, with all the noise, chaos, cheerful togetherness, and intimacy. We talked about the children, their names and ages, their likes and dislikes, my travels, and my grandchildren, and about Brexit, of course. Leah's family is just as divided as mine on that matter.

"I hate to see what's happening to this country!" I raved. "It's a disaster! Like lemmings jumping mindlessly over cliffs."

"Well, Helena, that's what is called democracy," Howard said rather condescendingly. "It's the will of the people. Surely you don't think that most people are mindless?"

"Yes, the will of misinformed and misguided people." Cheryl snapped.

"No, there are solid reasons for it." Howard patiently explained. "The country simply cannot cope with the ever-increasing influx of immigrants and refugees, can it?"

"But, Howard," I said, "you yourself are a child of refugees."

"That's different", he contested. "My parents and grandparents were educated and ready to work, to make their own way."

"But most of today's immigrants are making their own way." Leah joined in. "And we need them. Where would we be without Polish builders, overseas nurses, fruit pickers, and so on?"

"We don't need to be governed by some bureaucrats in Brussels!" Howard was getting exasperated. "That's no democracy!"

Our arguments went round and round in circles without getting anywhere - just like the Brexit negotiations.

"Time for the pudding!" Leah had had enough.

There was a delicious honey cake and a fruit salad with plenty of pomegranate seeds to bring a year full of good deeds.

At ten o'clock my cab arrived to take me back to Hendon Station. The driver was Italian, from Naples. He loved the sun and missed it badly, he said.

"But we have had a good summer," I protested. "Don't you think?"

"What summer?" he sneered. He was a poet. When he didn't drive cabs, he wrote poems. Oh, the Italian sun!

"Don't you want to go back to your sun then?"

"You must be joking. There is no work there. Youngsters roaming around in gangs killing each other. No, I can't go back to my sun."

"Well then, how about writing poems about clouds and rain, now that you are in England?"

He laughed and charged me eight pounds, quite a lot for such a short journey, I thought.

NOT MANAGING IN PRAGUE
2017

"I'm not managing" she used to say.
"That's because you are unable to say no," I'd say to her.

Dana would not only babysit at her children's beck and call, but she would also dutifully bring along a freshly baked cake or a salad, or a plate of homemade cookies for her grandchildren. Cooking and baking were usually done after work in the middle of the night. She always remembered people's birthdays and baked some more. She would cancel her plans because everyone else was needier than her. When she occasionally treated herself, there would be guilt.

"Come on, Dana, it's OK, enjoy it!"
"This menu is much too expensive, and little Bětuška needs new shoes."
"Your son can well afford to buy them for her."
"You know how busy they are."

When I phoned Dana, she would often still be at work even if it was late in the evening. She was a librarian and felt passionately about books and the importance of libraries. Her lazy, yuppie boss made good use of her dedication and gave her loads of work with impossible deadlines.

"I'm not managing."
"You must tell him it can't be done in that time."
"But our grants depend on it."
"Then he should give you a helper."
"That would only slow me down."

Dana was hard on herself, constantly underestimating her own value, her looks, her talents and her generosity. She was extremely conscientious. You could hardly find anybody more dependable and honest. She had a slight limp and perhaps because of her handicap she needed to prove she could do just as well as anybody else. Offering her any help was a bad idea; she would stubbornly refuse it. Inviting her out for dinner or just a coffee was almost impossible.

"Now I am in your debt."

"Dana, don't say that, it's my pleasure to treat you."

"I can't accept it."

"Why not? There is giving and there is taking, they go together. You are spoiling my fun."

How many times have I told her that? It was frustrating, it made me despair because giving any present would only cause her a great worry about how to recompense.

And so it went until she retired. Tragically, she was diagnosed with gallbladder cancer within a month of her retirement and died one year later. Even during her illness, she would still get upset about not managing. To walk as far as she would have liked, to bake twenty kinds of Christmas cookies instead of just ten, to finish knitting a jumper for Bětuška, to sort out her beloved books, to financially compensate her estranged husband. Dana's divorce was another cause for self-blame.

"Why did he leave? What have I done wrong? Where will he live?"

Dana inherited a small villa in the green southern suburbs of Prague. It was a basic but charming house with a small garden and a view of Prague Castle from the top floor. Dana's husband Vašek was a very good craftsman and worked hard to make the house comfortable and magical. They both put lots of love and effort into that house. There were homemade wooden benches decked by colourful covers, storage boxes shaped as fairy tale creatures. Lights festooned with crocheted decorations generated perplexing patterns on the walls. It was cosy, cheerful, and friendly. Dana knew her neighbours well and chatted to them across the fence, offering samples of her apricot jam or an apple crumble. At least she died in that house, surrounded by the families of her two children.

When Vašek left, Dana felt she must repay him for all the work he had done. She kept transferring large sums of money to Vašek's account, hoping that it would appease him and help her two children to inherit the house. So that the magic could continue. But soon after she had died, the house was sold to a property developer, and both of her children got divorced.

Last week, during my Christmas visit to Prague, I passed that house and remembered it was exactly ten years since Dana's death. Half of the house had been demolished already, the rest about to go. The cherished apricot tree was chopped down to make space for a much bigger and more upmarket villa. The apple tree was still standing but looked sickly and dejected. Who is going to live there next? Let's hope it will be a happy family, rather than one of those Russian wheeler-dealers who are buying properties around there. You can see their houses popping up among the solid 1920s family villas, obstructing views. Glass and steel, 'entrepreneurs' baroque'.

Enough of the gloom. The most wonderful thing about Dana was her sensitivity to others and her passion for things beautiful. Discussing with her our reactions to what we had just seen or heard was a joy. She responded to paintings, music or books with great perceptiveness and judgment, almost with a religious passion. Together we listened to Bulat Okudzhava's dreamy poetic songs. She introduced me to Vladimir Vysotsky's hoarse voice singing rebellious and angry Russian ballads, she swooned over Bob Dylan's records like a teenager in love. The stories she lovingly read to her grandchildren were carefully chosen, both for the texts and for the images. She liked tradition, history, and continuity. She wanted old customs to live on.

As I passed Dana's house, or what was left of it, I imagined myself visiting her, bringing a bottle of nice Moravian wine, leaving my footprints in the slushy snow, opening the creaky front door, changing my shoes for a pair of visitors' slippers that were always at the ready in the entrance hall.

"I love your Christmas tree! Did you make these straw angels?"

"Yes, but Bětuška made this one, isn't it good? You must taste my Beehive cookies, I made them this afternoon"

"Delicious!"

"Have some more! And try the Vanilla crescents too."

"I shouldn't, but I will. thanks. They are amazing."

"I'm sorry I didn't manage to bake your favourite black-and-white cookies this year but try the gingerbread ones."

"Perfect, I like the spicy flavor. So, how was your Christmas Eve?"

It's getting dark, but we are in no hurry. Dana lights the candles on the Christmas tree, I fill up our glasses and we talk.

Dana's Christmas Treats

OUR FRIEND IVAN
2018

The phone rings and I know it's Ivan because he phoned only five minutes ago, thinking I was Tim.

"Hello again, Ivan," I say, "Are you still trying to reach Tim?"

"It's my bloody phone!" he rages. "They are sabotaging it!"

"You could have dialled the wrong number. Do you want to try again?"

"No, it was Tim's number. Definitely. My phone just doesn't work. They have been doing it for years. They are messing me up."

I don't ask who is doing the messing. Ivan believes the secret services are after him. Persecution complex? Paranoia? Post-traumatic stress disorder? You name it, he has got it. And yet we all love our friend Ivan.

In his happier days, he used to walk the streets of London until small hours, observing countless "amazing coincidences". He ruminated over his findings and planned to write "The Theory of Everything", a great magnum opus that would explain the hidden connections between the physical and spiritual worlds. He always carried a heavy rucksack stuffed with books and scraps of paper that contained important messages and notes. He dragged it along through the night together with numerous plastic bags full of stuff to be taken home and sorted out later. His flat was bursting with it so that there was hardly any space for him. All of us who knew him wondered: "Where does he actually live?"

Besides the rucksack, Ivan also carried a camera, which he kept rolling on any occasion. "Hold it!" he would exclaim in the middle of a conversation and then thoughtfully arrange a few plates or flowers or postcards around the scene. The camera kept humming, aiming up and down and all around for hours, although none of us ever saw any results of his filming endeavours.

Ivan's council flat was broken in several times and obviously, that increased his anxiety. He believed that his flat was constantly under surveillance, irradiated, and bugged by secret services. Perhaps that's why he used to spend most of his nights on the streets.

Ivan could be badly depressed and enraged but often also in a state of euphoria, especially following observation of some happy occurrence. Such elation inspired his marvelous playfulness with words. Out of the blue, he could produce a most beautiful poem either in Czech or in English. He was well-read and saw associations and correlations in things and events that others did not notice.

His hair used to be long. Not just long long, but exceptionally, weirdly long. His heavy dreads reached the ground and then came up again to be tucked into his pocket. People stared, mostly angrily since it was not a pretty sight. Not a pleasant scent either.

"Why don't you cut your hair?" I asked him many times over.

"It's very complex", he would say, "I'll write an explanation for you".

But he never wrote one, just like he never wrote his "Theory of Everything."

My friendship with Ivan goes back a long way. We were fellow students in Prague in the 1960s. I studied biochemistry, he nuclear physics, and some of our lectures were joint. He was incredibly handsome, with dark curly hair and a devilish sparkle in his eyes. Unmissable. He entered university despite his difficult childhood circumstances. His father disappeared when Ivan was still a toddler, and an assortment of stepfathers followed. Ivan went through an ordeal of attending a couple of rather brutal children's institutions until he finally ended up in a boarding school where he was loved and encouraged. The sky was his limit - he chose nuclear physics, fascinated by the ambivalence of matter. During the heady days of the "Prague Spring," Ivan was highly active, organising happenings, discussions, and demonstrations, and often arrested and interrogated.

After the Soviet invasion of Czechoslovakia, we both ended up in England. He was stripped of his Czechoslovak citizenship and suffered his exile more traumatically than anybody else I knew. In his spirit, he never really left the country. We visited him in Cambridge, where he lived with his beautiful willowy partner and their two children in a chaotic but seemingly happy household. There Ivan continued with nuclear physics. But politics and activism took precedence, and he never finished his studies. Our children were of a similar age. The children played, the adults talked, it was fun to get together. But Ivan's relationship ended dramatically in the late seventies. His willowy partner disappeared with the children to an ashram somewhere in India and eventually ended up in California. I think it was then that Ivan stopped cutting his hair.

Ivan relocated to London and continued with political activities. Not officially, but in an alternative way: helping the homeless by occupying and claiming empty council apartment blocks, helping the Czech Underground groups by publishing their texts, organising support, and promoting Czech Rock groups such as "The Plastic People of the Universe". When in a good mood, Ivan was a star, the life of a party. Witty, entertaining, well-informed, sparkling, and ready to endlessly discuss anything under the sun with great enthusiasm and mischief. There was brilliance, but no outlet for it. Ivan was a great talker but not a man of action; he was unable to introduce any system into his constant flurry of ideas. He couldn't cope with the practicalities of life. Most of the letters he received remained unopened unless they were dealt with by one of his unfortunate girlfriends, by his daughter (from faraway America), or by his friends.

In the late nineties, the situation in his flat became untenable. It was a health hazard. Ivan insisted it was his private gallery, an artistic creation where every piece and its location had significance. But the council demanded he must clear his flat out. In desperation, Ivan asked for help. His children arrived from California; they were in their late twenties at the time. Another young man arrived from Prague: he was the son of a Czech dissident and was eager to work hard to help his father's friend in need. My friend brought a car and a huge number of outsize plastic bags – we were all ready to help. Wearing face masks and gloves, we spent some three hours in Ivan's 'Art Gallery', filling the bags and taking them downstairs. It didn't seem to make any difference to the place, and Ivan just paced up and down looking increasingly unhappy.

"How would you feel if I came into your house and started to throw your things away?" he shouted angrily. He could not bear it any longer. "Enough," he said. "Let's go to a pub."

And so, we did. Gradually Ivan regained his composure. For the next three hours, we sat and chatted about this and that. After a few days, Ivan's children returned to California. The confused son of the Czech dissident went back to Prague. Nothing was resolved and, for another decade, Ivan continued to haggle with the council about his Gallery.

Ivan reciting his poems

Ivan had many artist friends and acquaintances. His enthusiasm and feeling for arts and literature were ever-present. One of his friends, perhaps his best friend, was Sumeet, a down-

and-out gloomy Indian painter who was married to Chitra, a glorious Indian woman from high society. Sumeet's marriage fell apart at about the same time as Ivan's, but that's another story. Ivan and Sumeet would often come with their children to visit us at our first house in Croydon. I would cook huge quantities of spaghetti Bolognese while the children, six of them, played. The men talked. And talk they did. With time, Ivan's hair got longer and longer, my life busier and busier and my patience shorter. The visits became less tolerable and less frequent. Eventually, Ivan's lifestyle took its toll. His bad moods, anxiety, and anger became more prevalent. He would often shout and bang his fists on the table: the whole world was out to get him including his friend Sumeet. All the same, when Sumeet got ill Ivan looked after him with touching devotion until the bitter end.

After nearly forty years of cajoling by family and friends, Ivan finally agreed to have his hair cut. Not just cut cut, but meaningfully and ceremoniously cut in front of a large gathering of friends and onlookers on the banks of the river Thames opposite his beloved Globe Theatre. By then, Ivan had had many health issues and had been hospitalised several times. His flat had been cleared by the council during one of his hospital stays, and some eleven tons of stuff disposed of. He is back there now, confused but struggling on and occasionally, still writing his poems. He is heavily dependent on his distant daughter who phones him every day and miraculously, with a bit of help from his friends, manages to organise his life from that distance. What a sad metamorphosis!

"Ivan, can you read out the number for Tim that you have just dialled?"

He does.

"This is my number, Ivan. You must have got them mixed up. Don't you think so?"

"I must have done."

"So, no sabotage then, OK?"

"No, not this time."

PEPI'S ELEGY

2018

Mist is trailing over the Kunětice Mountain. It's a bleak, foggy November morning, cold and damp. This solitary volcanic mountain dominates the Elbe plain in eastern Bohemia. On its top stands an ancient castle, and underneath is the Kunětice village with its cemetery. There the family of my brother-in-law, Richard, Pepi's father, have their tomb.

Pepi died of lymphoma aged 52. Seven people stand in silence around a hole in the ground, each in their own thoughts. A moment ago, Luděk climbed up the ladder, up from the family tomb where he had just deposited the urn containing the ashes of his cousin.

"Goodbye, Pepi," he said as he emerged from beneath the stone slabs.

Next to me is my sister Sandra, pale and worn out. She and her husband Richard stand well apart, unable to provide any comfort for each other. Between the two of them are Luisa, Pepi's sister, and Michiko, our sister-in-law. Luděk and his son Daniel are on the other side of the tomb.

The seven of us are staring into that grave, a raw and basic scene. I am thinking of Pepi's short but wonderful life. Penniless, but free. Protected from the worst adversities by his parents for better or worse. For better because there was always his parents' backup. For worse because such a backup was not exactly conducive to standing on his own two feet. Also, for worse because the pressure that he should "get a proper job" was ever-present. But his job was being Pepi, the dreamer, the painter, the Green Man of Jizera Mountains. Pepi had known the Janov village since he was just two months old. Like us, the previous generation, he used to spend his holidays there as a child. When he grew up, he transformed our family cottage into a messy but magical place. It was Pepi who kept the cottage going through snow and sleet and rain and heat.

He knew the mountains intimately, naming rocks and brooks, and telling stories about people who lived in the neighbourhood. It was a pleasure to walk with him. Walking and talking. There was never any lack of subjects. History of Janov and the surrounds. Family matters. He always liked to discuss those. Relationships, the impact of family life on self and others. And his paintings of course.

"What have you done lately?" I would ask, and he'd show me. What did I think? Which one could I relate to? He'd explain his experiments with colours or his current fixations and how he's working his way out through them. Some of the paintings were too heavily symbolic. Head-shaped mountains in red clouds or a bulging female - Mother Earth. "A bit too mystical for me," I'd tell him. "I like your portraits and jungle landscapes. I like your white feathery castles in the air and Amanita mushrooms, on which ecstatic elves dance under the crescent moon." He painted what may be called naïve art, sometimes quite sophisticated, sometimes less so, but always with a passion.

I put my arm around my sister's shoulder. What can be worse than losing one's child? In Pepi, Sandra had lost her closest family ally. Despite the discord between them, visiting her son in the mountain cottage was her comfort, an escape. Pepi was someone she could talk to. She was repeatedly shocked by the mess Pepi lived in. She cleaned and cooked for him, although Pepi grumbled and disapproved of these invasions into his privacy. But one part of him was grateful.

"Sandra," I used to tell her at regular intervals, "he is nearly thirty, forty, fifty! You don't need to do this."

But she continued the same ritual. After establishing some order in the house, she could relax, go for a walk, admire the scenery, and drop in for a chat at the neigbours. Time stands still in Janov. Her old childhood friends are still scattered around in the neighbouring cottages. Where will she escape now? What will happen with the cottage?

Luisa stands there sad and resigned. Only a year ago she herself had overcome lymphoma. Richard's brother, her uncle, succumbed to a similar disease. But Pepi disregarded any genetic links. He was convinced there was some kind of curse over the family. I hope Luisa has no such thoughts. I wish I could cheer her up.

We stand, stare, and contemplate, getting chilled to the bone. Finally, Luděk breaks the silence.

"Well, Goodbye Pepi," he says again, "I'll miss you."

We embrace each other and start moving slowly towards the cemetery gate.

"There are still three coffins down there," says Luděk, shuddering. "They didn't do cremations two centuries ago."

It was then that Richard's ancestors bought a farm in this region. They may have been Huguenots escaping from France, but these are unconfirmed rumours. After some hundred years, the farm had been sold and the ancestors moved further east to Moravia but still, all the family members had been buried in this tomb ever since.

"The coffins are nearly decomposed," Luděk says, "you can see the bones inside, it's scary...."

Practical matters are discussed now, the tomb must be covered again, the cemetery manager informed.

Kunětice Mountain and the Cemetery

"Helena, have you thought about what you want to do with your ashes?" Michiko, my sister-in-law, asks me quietly. She arrived from Berlin only yesterday just for the day, to be with us for the occasion.

"Oh, dear!" I sigh. "I've no idea. I have made a will, but it's no good. I requested my ashes to be scattered here and there as if it mattered. Do you think it matters?"

"Well, somebody must decide. Who else but you?"

"I need to change the will, but I don't know how. I wish there was a family place for our ashes like this one, under a mountain topped by a romantic castle. Don't you think it's nice? Perhaps it was some comfort to Pepi - knowing the beauty of the place where he'll rest. Much too soon, of course. Our family's ashes are all over the place." I feel a shiver down my spine, thinking of Auschwitz. "And what about you?"

"I think I want my ashes to be used for planting a tree. There are these green burial grounds, burial forests." Michiko likes the idea of her body being recycled. "But first we have to live, don't we?" she says. "Life is so beautiful. We live and we die and that's it."

Yes, that's it. We may leave behind a bit of work and perhaps some feelings in others, warm, cold, loving, indifferent - always perplexed.

Richard had booked us for lunch in a nearby restaurant. The outside looks modest and inconspicuous, but the inside is warm and cosy, with roaring log fire, and amazing food on offer. The mood lightens. We begin to smile.

We talk about Pepi's eccentric girlfriend. Zora, in her early forties, lives in a caravan up on the hill above our cottage. She feeds mostly on nuts and seeds. Before consuming anything, she carefully appraises food's spiritual energy. Good vibrations or bad ones? She is good-looking and sporty, with long dark hair and a distant gaze. Every morning she walks barefoot in the grass to cool her feet in the dew. She communes with nature, takes photos of sunrises, sunsets, and full moons, swims naked in the tarn, and wants to be free. She won't make any commitments.

At first, Pepi had found this lack of constancy painful. He was sure it was a reckoning for his own wavering with the previous girlfriend who lived with him for twelve years and he was the one who could not commit. "The symmetry of it is amazing," he told me. "Now the score is even."

He managed to be quite philosophical in his anguish. With time he got used to Zora. She was his Green Woman, she suited him in some way. He too didn't like to be bound.

"There isn't anyone better on these hills," he decided.

But Pepi's father, Richard, couldn't bear to have Zora around.

"She was a great comfort to him despite her idiosyncrasies!" we argued,

But Richard disapproved of her so fiercely that she had to stay away from this family gathering.

And what about the healer that Pepi visited last summer? Our reminiscences continue. Again, Richard had no time for such things. He was a doctor; he knew there was no hope. But Luděk maintains Pepi felt much better after he had visited him.

"That afternoon, he laughed with all his heart at some silly jokes. He was in such a good mood. At least psychologically, the healer helped him," Luděk insists. "I know it's not logical, but what about comfort?" he asks. "Consolation has nothing to do with logic."

In his last year, Pepi felt more like writing than painting. We discuss the book of stories he published shortly before he died. He was remarkably stoical about his illness. "Hard work", he said about the book, "but I like a new challenge". Hilarious drunken tales, descriptions of comical encounters at home and abroad, wanderers' stories. His friends gave him a lot of support with writing and publishing. The book came out just in time: a gift from his friends to Pepi, and from Pepi to his friends.

We giggle as we remember these tales and as we order our mouthwatering food. Roasted goose, duck with red cabbage, garlicky rabbit with spinach, and the traditional schnitzel with potato salad.

It's only two o'clock in the afternoon, but the full stomachs, dark heavy clouds, cold, and mist make it feel like bedtime already. Moreover, everyone has things to do.

"Time to go," says Luděk. He and Daniel will be travelling towards Brno where they are running a family company, packaging and printing.

"We have a business meeting early tomorrow morning and need to prepare for it."

"Can you give me a lift to the train station?" asks Michiko. "It is on your way, isn't it? I must be back in Berlin tonight. My daughter Izumi is coming with her family tomorrow." She smiles happily. "I'll see my little grandson again! I am going to cook a Japanese feast for them."

"No problem," says Luděk, and off they go.

"So – that's it," says Sandra, unwittingly repeating Michiko's words. She fidgets in her handbag, looking for the car keys. "Oh God, where are they? I'm too tense. Richard, please," she hands him the bag. "Let's get home quick. I should be preparing a talk for Monday. Should I cancel it?"

We all think she should.

"I'll see how I feel," she says.

Richard found the keys and is driving us home.

"The fridge is full of that wild boar meat," he says. "I shall have to process it."

"From another grateful patient, is it?"

"Well, yes, it's a present from Johnny. I treated him ages ago. A triple bypass. He still remembers me every hunting season."

"How nice!"

"I'm going to prepare some portions for freezing and some of it we'll have for lunch tomorrow."

"Roasted vegetables would go very well with it, I'll prepare them." I'm trying to be of some use.

"I'll cook a soup for starters," says Luisa. She will stay a few more days with her parents doing her best to keep their spirits up.

I'll also stay the night. We'll look at Pepi's paintings, the house is full of them. Sandra, Luisa and I will go for a walk before lunch, it's easier to talk when walking. Not that one can say very much. I am here, Sandra. I'll be off to London after lunch, but I'll phone. We'll Skype. We'll email. I'll be back in six months. Let's plan a holiday together.

CAFÉ SOCIETY – A GUIDE FOR TOURISTS
2019

Cakes arranged artfully on lace paper doilies, armchairs upholstered with red velvet, and pedestal tables covered with round glass tops. Who needs a square meal? In Vienna, you have cakes for lunch and cakes for dinner. The choice is inexhaustible. A Konditorei at every corner. You enter these palaces of indulgence to be hit by the aroma of roasted coffee mixed with the sweet smell of caramel. A riot of colours greets you on the counter, a cornucopia of shapes and textures. Choose carefully. Consider the mood and the company you are in and make a good match.

The famous Sacher Torte is deceptively simple. Its rich dark chocolate coating hides inside a subtle dialogue between the slightly bitter cocoa and a sharpish apricot jam. A generous dollop of snowy cream provides contrast and sophistication. Eat it slowly, sip your mocha coffee, don't rush. Sachar Torte goes well with a bit of secretive gossip, but perhaps you would rather call it a discussion about relationships.

Or you could go for a more rustic apple strudel. Here the dialogue is between the soft, tart, juicy inside, and the crispy, crunchy outside. The pastry is dusted lightly with icing sugar; a scoop of walnut ice cream is slowly melting on its side. Don't dawdle, you don't want the ice cream to melt completely. Taste the apples, raisins, and cinnamon, and think of the golden autumn days. Orchards are overflowing with fruits. Piles of succulent shiny apples under the trees demand to be picked up and used. There will be strudels galore. The portion is huge, it will keep you going.

This food is made by and for hearty farmers. You may want a robust mug of coffee with it, rather than a delicate cup. But why not make it an Apple event? Consider a glass of semi-sweet apple cider. Strudels go well with a conversation about children and grandchildren, cats and dogs, walks, and weather; nothing too heavy. Relax, strudels are for comfort.

If you must talk politics, choose a companion with a different point of view so that you can practice your debating skills. An assortment of colourful mini cakes will be useful here: fruit cups, moose cups, mini eclairs, whirls and tartlets, mini gateaux, little meringue kisses, or finger doughnuts. Tell your opponent what you think and then listen attentively to his or her argument while you, at intervals, pop the chosen morsel into your mouth. If you agree, choose a soft and succulent piece that's easily consumed. If you disapprove, something hard and crunchy, eaten noisily, will help you to show your displeasure. Or something unmanageable, messy, runny, and dripping down your chin. That will clearly indicate your disagreement. You will need lots of cakes to give you strength for the debate. Any alcohol of your choice will do as a complement. Don't scrimp, the talking will go on forever.

If you just need someone with whom to share a good moan about the state of the world, you may be better off visiting Prague. You know you will practically make each other cry talking about Brexit, Boris, Trump, Putin, global warming, plastic islands, floods, tornadoes, fires, tipping points, and polarisation of the society; no lack of topics here. Prague cake shops or "Cukrárnas", will provide you with the cakes that are most suitable for such conversations. The coffin-shaped cakes filled with cream, traditional Czech desserts, are called "rakvičky ", which means little coffins. You don't want to spend too long a time weeping. One or two little coffins per person will be plenty. Turkish coffee accompanies little coffins very well and it will give you strength for a postprandial walk in a beautiful hilly park overlooking Prague. A walk much needed to lift your spirit up from the coffins to the spires and bridges of the magic city.

In London, searching for good cake shops is challenging. The English Café Society has not caught up with Middle Europe quite yet. There are very few pastry shops around. If you do find one, it will usually be called a "Patisserie". You may find it more beneficial, both for your taste buds and for your health, to hop on your bike together with a bunch of sporty men and women in lycra, and head out into the countryside. Tea Room Touring is a peculiarly British pastime. Its reward is the pleasure you will experience while enjoying the contrast between the blood, sweat, and tears of the road and the comfort of the cosy quirky tearooms with homemade cakes, lovingly baked on the premises and served on quaint chinaware. A conversation about gears, punctures, saddle sores, or narrow escapes from passing lorries goes very well with warm scones covered with jam and clotted cream, hearty tea loaves, fruit bread, and endless pots of well-brewed tea. Some of you may prefer to simply drive in a car from one Tea Room to another. The choice is yours but beware, the excitement won't be the same.

Cafés and cakes of Rome, Athens, and Istanbul will be explored next. Watch this space.

THE LYCIAN WAY
2019

Our Turkish guide was miles ahead. Light-footed Bez walked sprightly over roots and rocks, Kurdish scarf tied around his head, stopping at intervals, sometimes of his own will, sometimes after Neil, our English guide, had shouted to slow him down. Waiting obligingly for his flock to catch up with him, he would take pictures, light a cigarette, sip water or just scan the coastline with his approving eyes. Rocky cliffs, Aleppo pines, colourful spring flowers, azure skies above the distant snowy peaks, and the turquoise sea.

Towards Gelidonya Lighthouse

"No worries, no drama, all good!" Bez smiled when I had finally caught up with him, still puffing from the exertion of the climb. That was his favourite mantra.

"Beautiful isn't it?" I said.

"Çok güzel! That means very beautiful in Turkish. Turkish people don't walk, they don't know what they are missing."

"And what does your name mean, Bez?"

"Oh, it is actually a Persian name, Behzad. It was the name of my father's best friend. He was an Iranian pilot who died in an air crash. I was named after him. It means 'of a noble family'. I don't like it. I wanted to change it, but it's too late now."

"Don't change it. It suits you."

Whenever I managed to keep up pace with him, I learned a little more. It was hard work but worth it: my walking improved, and Bez's character and history began to emerge.

"How old are you, Bez?"

"Forty-five."

"Just like my son! How old is your mum?"

He hesitated but answered after a while. "Fifty-eight."

"She is just a baby! She must have been a teenager when she had you!" Oops, I put my foot in it, but Bez wasn't disturbed.

"Yes, she is young. But I am worried about her, she isn't well. Cancer, diabetes."

One day at Ölüdeniz Beach, Bez asked our group to sing the Happy Birthday song for his nine-year-old daughter. He filmed us and sent the file to her. She was chuffed to have been serenaded by Englishmen and Bez beamed as if he had just climbed Mount Ararat. He has another daughter, one year younger. Bez said the girls are looked after by his mum, so I assumed he must be divorced.

"Where is their mum, Bez?"

He waved his hand and said nothing.

The next day we were coming down a very stony slope. It was tricky but less demanding than climbing up, so I could just about keep up with him.

"My wife died," he said.

He told me that the girls' mum was called Klora. She lived with the family since her teenage years; Bez's parents took her in after she had become an orphan. Klora trained as a teacher together with Bez's sister, and the two girls became inseparable, like two sisters. Bez also thought of Klora as his sister. Besides, he was in love with a French girl whom he met at the beginning of his tourist guide career. However, after he had introduced the French girl to the family, his parents absolutely prohibited any further contact, causing him lifelong heartbreak.

Bez's sister and Klora liked to spend occasional weekends in the country and Bez accompanied them on various outings. One evening they were sitting on the terrace by the sea, watching the sunset and its reflection in the sea. Turks have a special word for it – 'yakamoz'. They were chatting, looking at the yakamoz, and Bez asked Klora "Why don't you get married?" She answered, "I would marry if I met someone like you." And Bez, without having had any previous thoughts about it, proposed to her there and then. Klora gave birth to two daughters, but soon after the younger girl had been born, she became ill. She had pains but kept quiet about it for far too long. By the time her breast cancer was diagnosed, it was too late to do anything. Bez was tortured by guilt. He could have been a better husband; he drank and was away from home frequently, perhaps trying to forget the French girl. One day his drunkenness caused an accident: he spilled some boiling water over the little girl's foot. From then on, Bez turned to religion and became a devout Muslim. It changed his life entirely, he said.

During our bus journeys, one could occasionally hear Bez's praying while he listened to the recitations on YouTube. When he didn't pray, he talked non-stop and very loudly to our driver Kadir. The two men stood in complete contrast. Kadir was tall and skinny, always calm, quiet, and slightly amused by us tourists. He was from Cappadocia, already a grandfather although he couldn't be more than fifty. His son got married two years ago; there were 1200 people at the wedding.

"Oh really?"

Yes, that's normal in Turkey. This summer it will be his daughter's turn – again about a thousand guests are expected.

Kadir tried to teach me Turkish. Every morning, as we were getting into the bus to be taken to the start of our walk, we had a little ritual:

"Günaydın! Good morning!" I would say.

"Günaydın! Nasılsın?" answered Kadir. How are you? Patiently, he waited for my reply.

"Teşekkür ederim. Iyiyim." I stuttered.

"Sen bir bomba!" Kadir encouraged me. You are a bomb!

Bez and Kadir work and travel together often. They were good friends, and Bez knew he must give Kadir some peace. Now and then, he would sit at the back of the bus. Bez was charming but overwhelming, noisy, and explosive like a bubbling volcano. Hyper.

"People often think I must be on drugs," he said. "Especially when I'm dancing. I love dancing, I go mad!"

"Omm" I chanted. "Calm down."

"Yoga isn't for me", he laughed. "It's too psychological, I need action."

"But there is a lot of action in yoga," I protested.

"No way, it's only psychology."

Bez was opinionated, sometimes surprisingly so. He said he now lives for his two daughters only. He'll make sure they study and marry the right men.

"How do you know who the right men for your daughters are?"

"They must be men with similar backgrounds."

His family comes from southeast Turkey, somewhere near the Syrian border. The right men must have the same traditions, same aspirations. Bez will never allow his daughters to marry any foreigners, no Europeans, Americans, Australians, no way. Not even any Turkish men from the Mediterranean, since they had already been spoilt by foreign influences.

"But Bez, you know what it's like from your own experience. How could you force the girls? They may meet someone at the university, fall in love…"

Oh no, Bez will make sure any potential suitors are introduced to him so that he can check them out. They can meet his girls, of course, go out, and talk, but no physical contact before marriage, not even holding hands, oh no. They must treat his daughters correctly. Otherwise, he'll beat them up.

Bez jumped and waved his arms to show how he would beat up any misbehaving suitors.

With Europeans it's always the same, he said. They are OK for the first five, seven, perhaps even ten years, but then, bye-

bye, off they go. And by then, he would be much too old and weak to punch them. His daughters would end up unhappily, fighting for the children and who knows what else. With local lads, he can be in control.

Our group devoted considerable time to discussions of these inconsistencies. To start with, Bez seemed so modern, at ease with us, touchy-feely, flirty, and assured.
"No worries, no drama, all good!"
Under his guidance, ruins of ancient cities emerged miraculously in the middle of forests, on deserted beaches or even under the sea. He talked with confidence, sometimes perhaps unjustified, but always charming, about tombs and sarcophagi, aqueducts and amphitheatres, agoras and odeons. Bez was happy when darting through the pine forests that were full of colourful wildflowers, irises, asphodels, and anemones. He scampered easily on stony paths cut into steep cliffs that sloped towards the pristine sea, cliffs covered with an abundance of yellow euphorbias. He knew the Lycian Way backward and forward and always found alternatives when a bridge was missing because of the earlier floods, or when the planned-for restaurant was closed.

Bez spoke forcefully against the present ultra-conservative president and his dynasty. Two years ago, his own brother had been jailed for seven years only because of a comment he had made on Twitter against the president. Bez thought their mother got unwell because of this. It was too stressful for her.
So much of Turkey's complexities seemed to be mirrored in this fiery person. I wanted to know more about his parents. His father died when Bez was still a teenager. He was a Zaza.

"What's that? I never heard of it."

"They are people from eastern Turkey, about 2 million of them. They have their own Zaza language, related to Kurdish. My mum is Kurdish. She doesn't speak a word of Turkish."

"Not a word of Turkish? Really? After all these years?"

Bez gave me a long hard look. "OK," he sighed. "I'll explain it to all of you."

It was the last day of our Lycian Way Ramble. We were just approaching yet another ancient ruins, those of the Roman city Phaselis. We were joking about 'the ruins again!', looking meaningfully at each other: some of us were rather getting on. Bez stopped us before we reached the magnificent aqueduct.

"I want to tell you something about Turkish minorities. There are many of them: Armenians, Greeks, Jews, Arabs", he paused and surveyed our group to see if we were interested. We were, and he went on about the named minorities for a while. And then: "Kurds are the largest minority by far, some fourteen million of them, nearly twenty percent of Turkey's population. My father was a Zaza, my mother is Kurdish. Zazaki and Kurdish are both Iranian languages, similar but different. That's what we spoke at home, Zaza and Kurdish. My mum doesn't speak a word of Turkish and some of you wondered why. Well, it was her own decision. One day in the 1980s, Turkish police came to our village, looking for something or somebody. It was shortly after the military coup, after which the Kurdish language was prohibited. I was about six years old and remember it well. They came to our house and shouted at my mother; she didn't understand and replied in Kurdish. One policeman hit her, and she fell. So that's why. After that, she never spoke a single word in Turkish."

We stood there, silent.

"No worries, no drama, all good!" Bez said finally. "Let's go and look at the ruins."

FAMILY REUNION IN THE TIMES OF CORONA
2020

My screen flickers as participants' panels slowly appear. The first two are my sons, Matthew and Oliver. Then Izumi, my niece, comes into view. Finally, we are joined by Izumi's father, my brother David, now known as 'Venerable Dharmakara.' This Buddhist name was given to him at his ordination some thirty years ago. Five panels, five different places in this world. Aberystwyth and Llanidloes in Wales, Frankfurt in Germany, Malá Skála in Czech Paradise, and Bromley in England. So much for the family reunion planned for Easter 2020 in London.

    The planning part of it had been easy: agree on the dates, click, and book your travels, all ready to go, Bob's your uncle. On my side: click to book a mega delivery of food, and then cook large quantities of the family's favourite dishes. I wanted to be free from cooking when we got together.

    Sadly, the dishes have stayed in my freezer. With the Coronavirus pandemic and social distancing, all our plans came to nothing. I'll be eating chicken paprika, apricot lamb stew, and roasted vegetable filo tarts for the rest of the year. A virtual reunion will have to do.

    In Frankfurt, Tomi hurls his teddy bear across the room and kicks his mother in the shin. Izumi smiles at us apologetically as she asks her two-year-old son to say hello to us, to the panels on her laptop. But Tomi pushes the laptop away and keeps shouting. As he runs in and out of the picture, Izumi speaks to him softly and patiently in Japanese. Then she switches to English.

"He's upset," she says. "His friends won't play with him anymore."

"Poor Tomi." We all sympathise.

"Our neighbours' children used to play with Tomi every day," Izumi sighs. "Now their parents pull them away when we meet on the stairs. How can I explain social distancing to a toddler? He can't understand what quarantine is, can he?"

"Why all this fuss?" David - Dharmakara intervenes. "Isn't it just like flu?"

"We don't know enough about it yet," Izumi tells him." Tomi pulls at her sleeve and shouts; we can hardly hear her now.

When she was a child, Izumi used to play the piano very well. It was her mum's ambition to make a world-famous pianist out of her. However, Izumi didn't like the pressure. She wasn't keen on listening to her father's guidance either. On his occasional visits, he always instructed her to study, whatever it was, very hard. Izumi dropped piano and decided to study law.

Now, Izumi and her husband Helmuth live in a solid apartment block in a lively and thriving area of Frankfurt. Both of them are lawyers. For the time being, Izumi has stopped working to take care of Tomi but she still looks the part with her outsized glasses, petite figure, and trendy clothes.

Dharmakara smiles at his lawyer-daughter and his grandson. His look is half bemused and half embarrassed. As if he knew something we don't. As if he had no idea how to relate to them.

"Hello Tomi," he tries. "Talking like this is difficult, I can't hear. What can we do?"

Suddenly, he goes muted and we can't hear him at all. He beckons to a young man, his disciple, who sits close by, ready to assist him. His sound comes back.

"Hello Tomi," David – Dharmakara tries again, but there is no response from the child.

Luckily, Helmuth now appears on the screen. He is coming down to the kitchen to pacify Tomi so that we can talk undisturbed. Helmuth is kind and quietly brilliant – we all think Izumi made a good catch. He sits down with Tomi on a parquet floor, opens a picture book, and the boy calms down immediately.

"Thank you, Helmuth!" I wave my hand at him.

"Poor Tomi," the conversation re-starts. "He must feel rejected."

"He must be traumatized. Dumped by his friends! That's so hard on him!" Matthew In Aberystwyth strokes his chin stubble as he speaks. Now that he is self-isolating, he works from home and has become quite casual about his shaving.

"Yes, that's right," Izumi agrees. "Tomi is really traumatised. He sleeps very badly and cries at night. Helmuth had to move upstairs to the spare bedroom. He needs silence to get some sleep. Otherwise, he couldn't work."

"I have heard that the parks in Frankfurt have been closed down," Matthew says. "I would go crazy if I couldn't get out. At least I can cycle to the top of Plynlimon Mountain to meet Oliver and his family. It's about halfway between us." He laughs. "Not sure if that's allowed, the regulations are so vague. We don't hug to be safe. We just say hello, and keep apart, but we enjoy a picnic together."

We use momentary peace to exchange information about our home-bound activities. Spring-cleaning, decluttering, gardening. Building a shed, mending a fence. Reading, watching movies. Walking in a park, taking elaborate side-steps upon meeting anyone in order to keep the prescribed 2m distance. No hugging, no jolly meals together, no visitors, no trips to shops. Little ordinary pursuits are suddenly valued and badly missed. On the other hand, there are the benefits of the slower pace of life. We don't need to be here and there and everywhere at a given time. With less traffic noise, we can hear the birds singing. The air is cleaner. Less rushing, less running fast to nowhere. More time just to breathe and feel alive.

"My life hasn't changed much," says Dharmakara. "Except that I can't travel so I now teach about Buddhism online. But I need some help with that, I am no good with computers." He laughs, looks at his disciple, and then makes another attempt to attract his grandson's attention. He waves to him awkwardly. But Tomi wants his mother now and starts crawling all over her.

In Llanidloes, Oliver's three children squeeze themselves into the camera's field of vision, make funny faces at Tomi, and wave their hands, but to no avail.

"Why don't you bring Bambi?" Oliver suggests. Before long, the eldest, his fourteen-year-old daughter, appears, clutching the cat to her chest.

Tomi's eyes light up as he stares at the cat.

Last summer, Izumi brought Tomi to Wales to meet his cousins. Oliver's three children fell in love with Tomi and Tomi fell in love with Bambi. The cat made a huge impression on him; he kept mentioning her name every day. A large photo of Bambi is stuck to the fridge in Frankfurt. Tomi points to the picture and then talks at the laptop.

"Bambi, Bambi!"

"Yes, there she is."

"Meow!" Bambi meows obligingly as if she understood.

A screaming little rascal changes briefly into an angelic smiling toddler, mesmerised by the quivering screen. But far too soon Tomi realises that the Welsh cat is not coming out to play in Frankfurt, and he rapidly changes back into his unhappy restless self.

A teacher friend of mine has told me that online teaching during the Corona pandemic has much improved her rapport with students. This generation of kids is so comfortable with virtual communication that perhaps social distancing makes no difference to them. Digital kids. They text each other from their bedrooms, happily exchanging memes on Instagram. Maybe, as Tomi gets older, he won't have problems with virtual cats anymore. He will chase them with joysticks on his consoles or race them against the virtual cats of his virtual friends. He may even become a Digital Nomad. A Post-Pandemic Digital Nomad. Sitting in his minimalist apartment bubble, digitally travelling around the world to numerous video conferences, and taking an occasional break to use his slot in the gym club. Clicking to have all his goods delivered by drones. No touch, no biohazard. All his movements, consumption, and communications carefully monitored and filed for the common good. Or perhaps Tomi will become one of those environmentalists, in whom I have put my faith, and he will save the planet.

For now, the cat in Llanidloes walks off the screen. In Frankfurt, Tomi continues to shout and run around. It's impossible to talk anymore in this din, so we say our goodbyes.

"Ahoy brácho!" I shout. "So long brother! Bye-bye, everyone! Who knows when we shall meet again in reality?"

"Ahoy ségro! Ahoy there everyone!" David's face brightens. I think he likes it when we are brácha and ségra - like in the old times, bro and sis. He relaxes with that familiar mischievous smile of his, although it could just be a sign of relief. This, for him rather uncomfortable, virtual reunion is over.

"You can all come and visit me here in Czech Paradise, there is enough space here for everyone."

"We would love to," says Izumi.

"Tomi would like it here. We could go boating on the river Jizera and there is an old castle Frýdštejn nearby."

"That sounds good. We could all have a reunion there." Izumi translates David's invitation into Japanese for Tomi.

We wave to each other and click the red buttons on our screens.

Bambi won't play in Frankfurt

A MOVING STORY (A BLOG)
2020-2021

MOVING OUT (1st Dec 2020)

You can't cheat your body. You may think you are in control, but your body knows better. You are scared, nervous, wondering what the hell you are doing. That last day of November, that morning when I was waiting for the removal people, my body displayed severe emotional diarrhoea symptoms. Like travel nerves, but worse. I always get travel bugs, travelling just wouldn't be the same without them. But this time, it was much stronger. What if they don't turn up? What will I do?

They did. Three young and strong guys with two rather small vans, much smaller than I had expected.

"My stuff will never fit into those!"

"Don't worry" they said, "we are Polish, we'll manage."

And indeed, they finished packing and loading by half past seven. They chucked the garden tools and my Mariner bike on top of the plastic-wrapped mattresses and drove away. They even took my old Dawes bike for their own use, which made me very happy. I like restoring old things to life, finding a new home for them. And a new home for the old me too: my 75th birthday present.

After the three Poles and their two vans left, I felt exhausted. I had a room booked in Bromley Premier Inn. Staying in the empty house without any bed and linen was no option. Too tired to say my goodbyes in an appropriate ceremonial manner, I wandered, mumbling, through the empty rooms. I have spent nearly forty years here, loved both the house and the garden. The house was built in the 1920s. It was of a good and practical design, and I tried to maintain its character. Bay windows, stained glass, panelled doors, blue and white kitchen. The 1940s coloured glass "fly catchers" lights hanging on brass chains from the ceiling. The garden was semi-wild and magical, with the Ravensbourne River at the bottom; a "managed woodland." We used to have occasional bonfires there, accompanied by somewhat drunken singing. What will happen to it now? Walls will come down to create the inevitable trendy kitchen-diner, the front garden will be covered with concrete to make space for numerous cars, cherished golden yew hedges will be mowed down to establish a formal lawn. Bye-bye Bromley.

The taxi arrived much too soon. And of course, the driver had no idea that an emotional leaving ceremony was just taking place. He showed no empathy at all while I rummaged for keys, for a face mask, for calm.

In the times of Covid, the Premier Inn was unpleasantly deserted but pleasantly anonymous. Revived by an excellent fish and gherkin from the chippy opposite the Bromley South Station, I slept on and off. When awake, I talked to myself.

"I have done it! Never mind the lockdown!"
"What am I doing?"
"It's going to be all right."
"What a clever move!"
"It's not quite done yet, there are still many things that can go wrong."

The same wobbliness the next morning.
"That's it then. What am I doing? Bye-bye Bromley. No way back!"

I was fine once I reached Euston Station. I passed a sort of tent village in front of it. Some homeless, some High Speed 2 protesters. I felt embarrassed. Wouldn't they like to have my problems? The problems of a poor little rich homeless girl.

Still, I even felt elated once I got onto the train. "Here I go! The adventure begins…"

I was told by my solicitors to expect a phone call at 1 pm, a call that would confirm the house sale completion and the money in the bank. It didn't come. My solicitor did phone me, but only to say that there had been a delay. Problems with confirming the buyers' mortgage. More stomach-ache. All could still fall apart.

156

Everything else worked to plan: My son waiting for me at Newtown Station. The three Polish youths and their two tiny vans waiting at the Newtown 'Lock-Stock' Storage Place. The three Polish angels, Roman, Bojo and Konrad, were busy unloading. They did so as efficiently as they handled the packing on the day before. Cheerfully, they were hastening my journey towards this new phase of my life. To the new beginning and also to the ending. I had to be philosophical about it.

My stomach-ache continued since there was no phone call yet from the solicitors. Only at 5 pm, just before the banks' closing time, did the confirmation call come. Finally - the money was in the bank! I have done it! The most complicated and most important step. My Bromley house was now officially sold. A great relief and elation took over and I was giggling all the way as my son drove from Newtown to Llanidloes. My future house waited there, and I hoped that by Christmas I would be able to invite the family for a feast.

WAITING 1 (28th Dec 2020)

Four weeks have gone by since my arrival here. Christmas has come and gone, and I have not moved in yet. I had assumed the process of buying would be a simple one: Both I and the sellers were not involved in any chain. I had the money. The house was empty; it was a legacy. My solicitor assured me there was nothing to prevent us from aiming for pre-Christmas completion. The moving-in date was set for December 18th.

However, none of us had considered the blatant incompetence and apathy of the Tax Office. They are not accountable to anyone. Communication with the HMRC and the Probate Office is a process so convoluted it would make even Kafka blush. Her Majesty's Revenue and Customs, the HMRC, started to deal with the legacy in August. Only after the sellers had written a complaint letter to their MP, things started to move a little: the mislaid tax receipt was finally sent to the Probate Registry. And that's where we are now, five months later. But the issuing of the Grant of Probate can take any length of time, three weeks or three months, nobody knows. I am not the only one who must put up with this. Serious Probate Registry delays are a norm. They are caused by IT issues, ineffective reorganisations of the Registry, massive backlogs due to excessive Covid-related deaths, and to a redeployment of staff at the HMRC onto Brexit-related projects. The problem was even discussed on 'You and Yours,' on Radio 4.

There was nothing for it: I could either withdraw from purchasing the house and start house hunting all over again, or I could live in hope while renting and waiting for the Probate Registry to act. Waiting with the knowledge that they are under no obligation whatsoever to do so. I have decided on the latter. To sort any new purchase out would take at least three months anyhow. Always look at the bright side of life. Relax, do plenty of yoga, go for walks, read, cook, zoom with friends, write something, be lazy. Easily said - if only I didn't have that niggling feeling that I should have a plan B. There was nothing certain at all about the house purchase, only a vague promise. Murderous thoughts, directed at Her Majesty's Revenue and Customs, would enter my head at night.

Meanwhile, it rained and rained, days were short and gloomy, the skies and the earth full of water. It flowed down from the hills in streams and rivulets, eventually entering the mighty River Severn, which speeds through the town of Llanidloes wild and forceful and menacing. The ground was muddy, soggy, and squelchy. I prized my boots out of the mud and continued walking. But there were a few moments, sometimes even an odd day, when bits of blue sky appeared, lush green hills glowed in the sun and the swirling clouds threw their shadows on them. Often a rainbow emerged here and there. Sun and water are regularly fighting it out in the air over the Welsh hills. When the sun comes out, the land looks so fresh and juicy, one almost wants to bite it. My daily walks kept my spirits up. Usually, I walked alone, trying to overcome my fear of dogs and other animals. But I am all right with sheep; they are everywhere. My London friends often ask me sarcastically: Have you seen any sheep? Have you counted the sheep yet? I suspect there is some envy lurking underneath. They are just walking around the same block day after day. With their face masks on.

The main reason for coming here was to be close to my family. My two sons and I have had a long-distance relationship for the last thirty years. When I wanted to see them, I would stay with them, and of course, they would stay with me when they came to Bromley. This is taken for granted in most Czech families, but not in Britain. Here people prefer to keep their distance. It was a shock to learn that the parents of my sons' partners wouldn't dream of staying with them when visiting. Not even for one or two nights. They preferred to book themselves into a hotel. The fear of interfering or being a burden choked the joy of togetherness.

Staying with my sons meant walking on eggshells, especially after they had married. Now I can pop in for a cuppa and then - goodbye and I go back to my guesthouse and eventually, I hope, to my house. No pressure. I can feel the difference already. Our interaction is much easier. Yesterday I walked with my granddaughter in the pouring rain, two blissful hours.

Yesterday, I also received a text message from a Bromley neighbour who is doing a bit of spying for me around my old house: The front garden gates and posts had been removed - ready for the concrete, I suppose. A big skip sits in the driveway, full of my blue and white kitchen furniture.

WAITING 2 (9th JAN 2021)

No development with the move could be expected during the festive season. Thus, there was nothing I could do in this matter, and I indulged in sweet inactivity. More phone calls to and from my friends, more zooming, watching films and documentaries. Reading. And continuing with the exploration of the countryside. These walks were crucial for maintaining my morale. I walked one to two hours on most days, soaking in the land and the skies.

Christmas Day and New Year's Eve were spent within the exclusive family bubble. That was quite a privilege since the rates of Covid infections were steadily increasing and the social restrictions were severe. A walk with the family to the source of the River Severn via Hafren Forest was very snowy. It was a welcome variation from my usual local loops. However, I kept reminding myself that I must not become a nuisance; the family needs time to themselves. More snow on New Year's Eve. The hilltops remained snow-dusted until now. White hills surrounding the juicy green vales, what more could one wish for? On cold frosty mornings, the white dusting was spread also over the valleys, and as it slowly evaporated, the rising mist created Fata Morgana- like images.

Five days ago, I had taken to bed feeling unwell. Could it be Covid? I worried. But there were other explanations. Not only had it been the coldest day so far and my room was freezing, but I had also had an upsetting post-Christmas telephone conversation with my solicitor. She said the delays in Probate Registry are immense and the wait could take months. I should start looking for another house. I do need a plan B. The cold, together with this shattering of my festive serenity, could have triggered the flu. I took two aspirins and slept for twelve hours. Feeling fine the next morning, I went for a long walk and then started searching for alternative houses on the internet. Five viewings were arranged for the coming Saturday, that is for today.

Last night, however, there was good news! The Grant of Probate was issued on January 7th (it took them 22 weeks!) and my solicitor said she expects to receive the written confirmation next week. So, I cancelled three out of the five viewings but kept two appointments. Just out of curiosity. As it happened, I fell in love with one of the two houses. A 1930s five-bedroom house in Newtown, only about 20 km away from Llanidloes, well modernised, easy to maintain, quiet, fantastic views, relatively cheap, no chain. I had no obligation to buy the Llanidloes house, which suddenly seemed much less attractive. I had to decide what to do next. It was a huge temptation because the Newtown house offered plenty of space for books, visitors, and perhaps even potential carers. Here, I could stick to my comfort zone, to what I was used to. But plenty of energy would be needed to manage it all. After an agonising afternoon, I returned to plan A. I don't want to spend my remaining energy on running a big house, I love Llanidloes. I love being close to my family. The time was ripe to downsize.

MOVING IN   24th Jan 2021

After receiving the Grant of Probate, things moved quickly. Exchange of contracts on January 15th, completion on the 20th, and the transfer of my stuff from the storage on the 23rd.

The plan was for me to move into the house on the night of the 20th with an air mattress borrowed from my son. It would give me time to look around and plan what goes where. My son Oliver would come after work to take me from the guesthouse to my new home. I was waiting for him in eager anticipation. As luck would have it, he had a burst tyre on his way home and was stuck on the road, waiting for an AA man. Meanwhile, storm Christoph hit Llanidloes with a vengeance. I was desperate to finally get to my new home, but how? Luckily, Paul, the other guesthouse lodger, had just got back with his large yellow rover and took me there with one armchair and the mattress. He was very helpful despite the raging rain. My daughter-in-law came along and eventually, my poor exhausted son appeared as well. We all had a good look around. Oliver pumped the mattress up and then they all left and here I was, all alone.

The first night was scary. Odd scraping sounds could be heard. A multitude of flies emerged from God knows where and congregated around lights. Buzzing flies, dead bodies....... Throughout this moving adventure, I often imagined I am actually arranging my own funeral. The ominous flies fitted the picture. I couldn't help thinking of Pam, the lady who had lived and died here. Doors squeaked, something rustled. Flies buzzed. To escape them, I switched the lights off and transferred the mattress to a dark room. I shut the door and listened to the noises.

The next two days were spent with my yellow rubber gloves on, cleaning the windows that had not been opened for years. The windows, where those bloody flies resided in nooks and crannies, assuming they were safe. How wrong they were! Their lives were cut short. And many other lives. Amazing how rich and varied life can be in undisturbed window recesses. I also cleaned the carpets upstairs before they would get cluttered by furniture. Spaces were measured, plans were made. All that activity pushed away the doubts and the fears. I was ready to start anew.

The storm Christoph had gone by Saturday 23rd; the Beast from the East arrived in its place. It was bitterly cold that morning, but sunny and bright. Much better for moving than the rain. Oliver drove me to the Newtown storage place and brought a much-needed thermos with hot ginger tea. The three removal men arrived, not the Polish ones, but Welsh, Alun, Blake, and Taylan. They came to the "Lockstock" stores with two vans which, yet again, seemed much too small. Yet again, the men managed to put everything in and were having much fun while doing so. They were joking non-stop as they lifted and carried, pretending to one another that light objects were heavy, and the heavy ones were light. Oliver's wife and children came to help with unpacking and all of us spent a most frantic afternoon. Surrounded by the family and the chaos, I began to feel at home. In the evening we could finally sit down on armchairs and sofas and admire our achievements. Tired out and in my own bed at last, I slept like a log.

Unusual brightness seeped through the curtains this morning. There was snow everywhere and not a cloud in the sky. Several juicy female pheasants were pecking around in the garden. A beautiful pheasant cock perched on the wall and watched them. Masses of snowdrops were already pushing through the snow. Later that morning Matthew, my other son, arrived from Aberystwyth. He sorted the heavy boxes with books into the garage to be unpacked later and helped with emptying the boxes with pots and pans and china. At the end of the day, we could treat ourselves to a dinner roasted in my new oven.

Looking back (28th February 2021)

After a month of living here, things feel right; the house, the closeness to the family, the countryside. I miss the company of course. It's like solitary confinement sometimes, but that is true for many of us nowadays. At least I have the 'family bubble' to interact with, just a twenty minutes walk away. We don't need to make laborious arrangements to see each other anymore. But it could have ended otherwise. What would have happened had I, as was my original plan, ended up in Shrewsbury? I dread to think.

I had considered Llanidloes to be far too remote. Nobody would ever come to see me there, I thought. I was also worried that the closeness to the family could cause tension. Shrewsbury seemed a good compromise: easily reached by train or car both from London and Wales. At the end of September, I travelled to Shrewsbury to find the house of my dreams. I had 22 'deceptively spacious properties in highly sought-after areas' on my list, and with the help of both my sons, we succeeded in viewing them all in just two days. I was not too impressed with Shrewsbury. It has a beautiful historical centre but also sprawling suburbs full of rather anonymous and disappointing houses. But there was one house that I liked. It was on a road adjacent to the Lyth Hill Nature Reserve. From what would become my future study, I could see Wrekin Hill. The pretty town centre with its rail station and other temptations was just 20 minutes bus ride away. Mornings, I would be jogging in the Nature Reserve. For the afternoons, there were galleries, museums, and coffee houses. Long Mynd was within reach; I could promenade there to admire the views of Shropshire Hills. I made an offer on that house and began to dream of my charmed life at the edge of Shrewsbury.

It was Oliver, who insisted I should at least have a quick look at a house in Llanidloes that, he thought, would be just the thing for me. We managed to squeeze in an early morning viewing.

I liked the house very much, but no, Llanidloes was far too remote. I stuck to my fixed idea.

I took my Shrewsbury dreams back to Bromley, booked a surveyor to check the Lyth Hill house, and started to pack for real. At the end of October, Matthew and Oliver came to help with the packing. That very same weekend, the surveyor phoned to report on the Shrewsbury house. Bad news. The house with the Wrekin Hill view was a mess. The surveyor mentioned just a few problems. He would send me a full list later. I should think hard, he said, do I really want to take it on? Utterly disappointed, I burst into tears. What shall I do? I had accepted an offer on my Bromley house already and was in the process of selling it. Nearly all my stuff was in boxes. In Wales, the 'short sharp firebreak' lockdown was just about to start. Matthew and Oliver would not be able to help me anymore. How could I look for any more houses?

We had to put a brave face on it. We continued packing in a gallows humour mode. There was not much point in discussing

166

the options, I would need to reconsider everything in silence. Totally stressed and unable to sleep, an idea entered my head in the small hours of Sunday. The house in Llanidloes! Why not? That would be the answer to this mess. My dreams switched with remarkable ease from Shrewsbury to Llanidloes. The charming, unpretentious market town with its proverbial market hall on chicken legs. Surely, I could manage the family situation, it would be all right, much better in fact. The abundance of fitted wardrobes in the house would be wonderful. From what would become my future study, I would be able to see Gorn Hill. And it is only one extra hour from Shrewsbury, that shouldn't put my friends, my real friends, off. But perhaps it had been sold already?

Matthew and Oliver had left on Sunday night, and I spent another sleepless night worrying about the house in Llanidloes: had it been sold already? I phoned the agent first thing Monday morning. The house was under offer, but the sellers have not accepted yet. I offered the asking price straight away and waited. The sellers accepted and the rest is history.

A BEAUTIFUL FOREST
2022

"Brexit," he shouted. "For me, that was the last straw. This country's getting more and more like the US! When I left, I was so happy to be able to live in Europe. But now….."

"Yes," she said. "It was a terrible disappointment. What a mess! And it's only going to get worse."

They walked on a muddy footpath; their conversation intermittent as they searched for dry patches between puddles. Unfolding leaves were covering the bare trees with delicate, pinkish-green lace.

He continued to list various misrepresentations and outright lies, on which the Brexit referendum vote was based, waving his arms around and getting more and more agitated.

"You are preaching to the converted," she said, but that didn't stop him. He continued to gesticulate. "What good has it done to anybody? It's so depressing!"

"Oops!" she exclaimed "I'm sinking!" One of her boots had got stuck in the mud.

"Are you all right?" He offered his arm, fulfilling the role that she assumed he assumed was the polite role expected of him vis-à-vis a woman ten years his senior. "Put your foot on this stone here, it's solid. Are you all right?"

"Well, my toes are wet, but only a little." She pulled her boot out and giggled but stopped herself straightaway. Too girly. "You were saying?"

"And all this nonsense about immigration! Now we have a serious labour shortage, how's that going to help the economy?"

"What can we do about it? I don't know." She sighed. "Not very much. But look! There are newborn lambs over there!"

He stopped to take a picture. "Yes, very rustic, cute. I must send a photo to my brother. Although I'm not sure why I should. He has practically forgotten I exist. He only contacts me when he needs money. Not that I've got any. I've given it all away. Not that I get any thanks for it either. I've been such a fool!" He began to laugh hysterically. "Such a fool! Giving it all away!"

"Would you like a sandwich? Those dry logs over there, we could sit on them and have a picnic. Have you brought tea?"

"Yes, let's do that. That's a good spot."

He pulled a large thermos out of his rucksack. She unpacked the sandwiches. Cheese and chutney, his favourites.

"Delicious," he said. "I always like your sandwiches. You know how much I appreciate it. And I love our walks."

"Thanks," she said. "I've also got some radishes and tomatoes."

"There was an amazing Jewish deli in New York, I used to get sandwiches there."

"In Prague, you can get little open sandwiches. They have got them everywhere and they are very decorative, and…"

"Pastrami, salted beef, salmon, and cream cheese. The smell alone, as you entered, made you ravenous. Oh, they were wonderful."

They sat at the edge of the wood, looking at the lambs, running around, bleating, and looking for their mums. One of the lambs seemed lost, bleating desperately but ignored. She kept quiet and hoped the food would lift his spirits. There was still a chill in the air; hot tea felt luxurious and comforting. He continued to describe the treats from the Jewish deli and then moved onto the

New York Chinese quarter where his friend had introduced him to a superb diner.

"Yes, your friend knew exactly what to order, didn't he? You must have had some wonderful feasts!"

"You bet! I so miss that Chinese diner."

"I miss those Prague bistros and delicatessens shops with open sandwiches…"

"You just can't find anything like that Chinese diner over here."

"….those garnished bread slices with a variety of ingenious colourful toppings.."

"Oh, and the Chinatown market on Bowery Street! Anything you need to cook a proper Asian meal! You just can't get these things here."

"London's Chinatown is pretty good."

"I don't know London very well. In London, maybe, but not here."

"No, not here", she agreed.

Never mind, she thought, let's live in the present. Here I am, venturing far into the countryside, despite my fear of dogs. Protected from those vicious animals by a guy with an excellent rapport with canines. Or so he says. He claims they don't worry him. Never mind that he could talk the hind leg off a donkey. Or off a dog, more likely. As if he were convinced the talking would set his troubled mind free. Well, perhaps it will…On his good days, he says how lucky he is to end up in this part of the world. Although he doesn't have a clue where he walks. Still, he is always happy to go.

"Would you like an apple? Or a piece of chocolate?" she offered.

"Chocolate? Oh, yes please, I can't say no to chocolate."

To some extent, we do have a similar perception of the world. His one is blue, a very dark blue, and mine is rosy – despite the bloody Brexit.

"What a beautiful forest," she said. "Awakening after winter. So subtle. This is the best time of the year, don't you think?"

"Yes, a beautiful forest!" Again, he laughed hysterically. "A beautiful forest, yes. You are right. Sorry, I keep ranting."

"No worries," she said. "It's fine."

Calm and rustic

AUTUMN IN LLANIDLOES
2023

A magnificent oak tree stands just behind my garden fence and spreads its massive branches wide and high. I can hear the oak whispering as I rake the fallen leaves. It is the sound of acorns making their way down through the foliage. This year, the acorn crop is unusually rich; the ground is covered solid. Gathering and transferring these acorns into the garden bin is a back-breaking effort.

Although I love the tree's whisper, I feel it is a bad omen, a warning. The world is falling apart. There is no end to dreadful wars. Global warming is out of control. Climate people say this year is likely to be the warmest ever. We are going to be extinct soon. Maybe that's why there are so many acorns this year.

I asked Google. The answer: an acorn-rich year is just a part of oak's irregular life cycle and is called a "Mast Year." It is certainly good news for squirrels and mice, and possibly also for oaks. Strangely enough, other trees undergo their mast years at the same time, apparently communicating with one another. "Let's have a mast year this year, shall we?" they call to each other. We still have no idea how and why they decide which year is going to be the one. But they can't have such fun every year, they would exhaust themselves by producing so much. So, that bad omen feeling is my very own.

There are sheep and two horses grazing on the meadow behind my garden fence. As I rake the lawn, sheep stare, and the horses come quite near to get a better look. They allow me to stroke their large thoughtful heads. I bring them some carrots and after that, they are my friends. Now they always come near when I do my gardening. "Have you got any carrots for us today?" A perfect idyl on my doorstep, extinction seems to be miles away from here.

One minute there is a downpour, the next minute the sun is shining, and a rainbow appears. Great weather for mushrooms. Some established themselves on the mossy front lawn under a snow-white Himalayan Birch tree. Even ceps, birch boletes and chanterelles! Beautiful and edible. Mushroom picking was very much part of my childhood; the resonance and the thrill these finds bring to me are impossible to explain to any locals; they have an ingrained fear of all fungi except those bought in supermarkets in plastic boxes.

When walking to the town, I make sure I take the river path even when it makes the journey longer. I don't want to miss the sight of the Severn, whether calm or rushing and raging, always appealing. I go to the town to shop, to catch a bus, to visit my family, and sometimes, not very often, to meet friends. Making new friends is not easy. There are friendly chats over the fence with the neghbours. "A good day for gardening!" we say to each other, or – more likely – "Will that miserable, bone-pervading rain ever stop?"

One can join various activity groups. There is a refugee support group I belong to. "You can't save the world", we comfort each other, "but you can help a family." We meet regularly, raise funds, and discuss what help is needed. There are also two

173

walking groups that I have joined and benefited hugely from their company. The members' superior knowledge of the surrounding countryside is an additional bonus. "How beautiful!", we sigh as we stride up and down the hills come hell or high water. "We must treasure each moment," we say to each other since most of us are already of that age when we must.

My digital photo album is full of pictures of sheep on hills with dramatic clouds towering above them. The clouds, together with the occasional piercing sun rays, produce exquisite light effects – fifty shades of green and rust. Who could resist such photo opportunities? Laboriously, I file my digital images and try to note down their unpronounceable origins: Llanwrthwl, Cwmcyndd, Llidiartywaun, Pistyllgwyn…..One day I will learn how to say it, perhaps even understand it.

Sheep and Hills

Printed in Poland
by Amazon Fulfillment
Poland Sp. z o.o., Wrocław